NEW DIRECTIONS FOR ADULT AND CONTINUING EDUCATION

Susan Imel, *Ohio State University*
COEDITOR-IN-CHIEF

Jovita M. Ross-Gordon, *Southwest Texas State University*
COEDITOR-IN-CHIEF

Facilitating Learning in Online Environments

Steven R. Aragon
University of Illinois at Urbana-Champaign

EDITOR

Number 100, Winter 2003

JOSSEY-BASS
San Francisco

FACILITATING LEARNING IN ONLINE ENVIRONMENTS
Steven R. Aragon (ed.)
New Directions for Adult and Continuing Education, no. 100
Susan Imel, Jovita M. Ross-Gordon, Coeditors-in-Chief

Microfilm copies of issues and articles are available in 16mm and 35mm, as well as microfiche in 105mm, through University Microfilms Inc., 300 North Zeeb Road, Ann Arbor, Michigan 48106-1346.

ISSN 1052-2891   electronic ISSN 1536-0717

NEW DIRECTIONS FOR ADULT AND CONTINUING EDUCATION is part of The Jossey-Bass Higher and Adult Education Series and is published quarterly by Wiley Subscription Services, Inc., A Wiley company, at Jossey-Bass, 989 Market Street, San Francisco, California 94103-1741. Periodicals postage paid at San Francisco, California, and at additional mailing offices. Postmaster: Send address changes to New Directions for Adult and Continuing Education, Jossey-Bass, 989 Market Street, San Francisco, California, 94103-1741.

SUBSCRIPTIONS cost $80.00 for individuals and $160.00 for institutions, agencies, and libraries.

EDITORIAL CORRESPONDENCE should be sent to the Coeditors-in-Chief, Susan Imel, ERIC/ACVE, 1900 Kenny Road, Columbus, Ohio 43210-1090. e-mail: imel.l@osu.edu, or Jovita M. Ross-Gordon, Southwest Texas State University, EAPS Dept., 601 University Drive, San Marcos, TX 78666.

Cover photograph by Wernher Krutein/PHOTOVAULT © 1990.

www.josseybass.com

5392935

EDITOR'S NOTES

Advances in technology during the last decade have brought challenges and opportunities to the ways in which individuals are educated and trained, in particular through online instruction. This Internet-based form of distance education delivery has changed the landscape of how instruction is designed, delivered, and evaluated. In addition, online instruction has redefined the role of the instructor in the learning process. Instructors do not "teach" in the traditional sense but now have increased responsibilities in course design and communication management.

Although online instruction is seen by many as a major breakthrough in teaching and learning, it still has its share of critics. Advocates of Internet-based education and training see it as a means for facilitating the exchange of information and expertise while, at the same time, offering opportunities for all types of learners in distant or disadvantaged locations (Hill, 1997; Webster and Hackley, 1997). Critics of this new form of instructional delivery do not believe it can actually solve difficult teaching and learning problems (Conlon, 1997) and believe that many barriers hinder effective online teaching and learning.

As part of a recent study, the literature review by Johnson, Aragon, Shaik, and Palma-Rivas (2000) uncovered several criticisms associated with online instruction. These included "the changing nature of technology, the complexity of networked systems, the lack of stability in online learning environments, and the limited understanding of how much students and instructors need to know to successfully participate" (p. 30). Additional criticisms included the Internet's threat of commercializing education, reducing standards, isolating students and faculty, and possibly devaluing university degrees. However, this same study, as well as the empirical study by Aragon, Johnson, and Shaik (2002), found promising results of online instruction.

In the former study, the researchers found that although student satisfaction with the learning experience is slightly more positive for students in a traditional face-to-face format, no difference exists in the quality of learning that takes place (Johnson, Aragon, Shaik, and Palma-Rivas, 2000). The distribution of course grades and the ratings of three independent, blind reviews show no difference in the quality of course projects across the two course formats. The results of this study support the argument that online instruction can be as effective as traditional face-to-face instruction if it is designed effectively.

In the follow-up study, Aragon, Johnson, and Shaik (2002) examined the influence of learning style preferences on student success in online and face-to-face environments. Although differences in learning preferences were initially found between the face-to-face and online students, these were not significantly apparent when student success was controlled. This was an important finding when, by design, online environments build significantly on reflective observation (learning by watching and listening) and abstract conceptualization (learning by thinking). The researchers conclude that students can be just as successful in online environments as face-to-face environments, regardless of their learning style preferences.

The ultimate concern for education and training is how to optimize instructional designs to maximize learning opportunities and achievements. The empirical research presented in the preceding section has showed that online learning can be as effective as face-to-face learning in many respects. It is the belief of these researchers, as well as each author contributing to this volume, that the development and use of online programs should continue. Although Johnson, Aragon, Shaik, and Palma-Rivas (2000) caution that practitioners who develop online instruction need to be familiar with the limitations of online programs, Aragon, Johnson, and Shaik (2002) state that "quality and thoroughness of the design and delivery must be the catalyst for ensuring positive learning experiences" (p. 243).

The purpose of this volume is to discuss ways in which quality can be established in online programs, whether in educational or noneducational settings. The volume begins with a discussion of specific characteristics associated with persistence, resourcefulness, and initiative in independent, autonomous learning. In Chapter One, M. Gail Derrick presents the argument that success in online environments is dependent on the role of autonomy in order to create sustained and enduring learners. She discusses her current research and identifies ways through which autonomous learning is established within the learning environment.

In searching for online programs, students typically ask two questions: What's in it for me? and Will it work? In Chapter Two, Seung-won Yoon discusses the idea that quality online programs are made up of a "blend" of technology, pedagogy, organization, strategy, and vision. Therefore, consumers of online programs need to go beyond asking simple questions and dig deeper into the structure on which the program is built. Yoon takes the stance that it is the right combination of these five factors that leads to meaningful online learning experiences for all key players.

Chapter Three presents a pedagogical model through which the design template for a master's-level online program was built. Scott D. Johnson and Steven R. Aragon make the case that instructional designers need ways to support quality teaching and learning within online environments that take into account the variability in student learning styles, provide external motivation for the isolated students, and build community, collaboration, and communication among learners. Johnson and Aragon present seven principles they believe establish powerful online environments.

The use of online instruction as a means of delivering education and training has changed many of the roles and responsibilities of the instructor. In Chapter Four, Adam D. Fein and Mia C. Logan discuss the new challenges and opportunities that the online environment presents to instructors. In response to the changing environment, the authors discuss strategies that can help instructors thrive within these environments.

In Chapter Five, Steven R. Aragon presents the concept of social presence as a significant factor in improving instructional effectiveness and contributing to a feeling of community among learners. Using a definition of *social presence* as the extent to which people in online environments are perceived as "real," Aragon discusses the benefits of social presence on student satisfaction and learning. Strategies for increasing levels of social presence in the online environment are presented.

Online technology initiatives have had an impact on the way student learning is assessed and evaluated. In Chapter Six, Angela D. Benson takes a look at how the use of online instruction has influenced what it means to assess and evaluate student outcomes. In this chapter, Benson discusses methods and approaches to student assessment and evaluation that are appropriate for these instructional environments.

The number of individuals completing degrees through online programs is growing rapidly. In Chapter Seven, Herbert E. Huber and Jean C. Lowry discuss their experiences as students who completed master's degrees online. The authors highlight the benefits and challenges of learning through this environment. They also provide recommendations to institutions for strengthening online programs, as well as to students considering an online program for degree achievement.

Finally, Lisa A. Garrett and Connie L. Vogt, in Chapter Eight, discuss the impact that online technology is having on the training and development initiatives of business and industry. In this chapter, the authors discuss how trends such as globalization, technology, demographics, economics, and the ever-increasing need for skilled workers have cultivated an environment open to online learning. Garrett and Vogt conclude the chapter with a case study from Intel Corporation, describing how online instruction has changed the way technician training is delivered and estimating the cost savings.

It is clear that online instruction is here to stay and will continue to serve as a primary means through which people receive education and training. Online instruction has the potential to reach a group of learners that possibly may otherwise remain excluded from educational and training opportunities that rely on traditional methods of delivery. I hope that this sourcebook provides new ideas and models for enhancing online programs already in existence. It should also provide pros and cons for those who are in the process of initiating or thinking about initiating online programs.

Steven R. Aragon
Editor

References

Aragon, S. R., Johnson, S. D., and Shaik, N. "The Influence of Learning Style Preferences on Student Success in Online Versus Face-to-Face Environments." *American Journal of Distance Education,* 2002, *16*(4), 227–244.

Conlon, T. "The Internet Is Not a Panacea." *Scottish Educational Review,* 1997, *29*(1), 30–38.

Hill, J. R. "Distance Learning Environments Via World Wide Web." In B. H. Khan (ed.), *Web-Based Instruction.* Englewood Cliffs, N.J.: Educational Technology Publications, 1997.

Johnson, S. D., Aragon, S. R., Shaik, N., and Palma-Rivas, N. "Comparative Analysis of Learner Satisfaction and Learning Outcomes in Online and Face-to-Face Learning Environments." *Journal of Interactive Learning Research,* 2000, *11*(1), 29–49.

Webster, J., and Hackley, P. "Teaching Effectiveness in Technology-Mediated Distance Learning." *The Academy of Management Journal,* 1997, *40*(6), 1282–1309.

STEVEN R. ARAGON *is an assistant professor in the Department of Human Resource Education at the University of Illinois at Urbana-Champaign, specializing in postsecondary education (community college), teaching and learning models for postsecondary minority and nontraditional students, and minority student development in community college settings.*

CONTENTS

ERRATA

On the cover and title page of *New Directions for Adult and Continuing
Education*, no. 99, the order of the editor names was incorrect. The
correct order is as follows:

Darlene E. Clover, Lilian H. Hill

1

Opportunities to engage in learning anytime or anywhere must address the issue of how to foster the desire for sustained and enduring learning. The need to understand the conditions necessary for facilitating this type of learning requires an understanding of the behaviors associated with autonomous learning coupled with self-efficacy beliefs.

Creating Environments Conducive for Lifelong Learning

M. Gail Derrick

A technological transformation during the past decade has eliminated the boundaries between formal and informal learning. As we adapt to a knowledge-driven society, a cultural transformation is occurring. Lifelong learning is an essential goal of education as a means to improve the quality of life for an individual, a culture, or a society. The value of sustained learning is demonstrated through changes in economic growth and social well-being, as well as the development of a democratic way of life. Although we now have opportunities to engage in learning anytime or anywhere, we must address the issue of how to foster the desire for sustained and enduring learning and, more important, create environments that are conducive to this lifelong learning process.

Establishing the conditions necessary for facilitating and enhancing the capacity for sustained and enduring learning requires understanding which behaviors are important for independent, autonomous learning. The research of Derrick (2001), Carr (1999), and Ponton (1999) establishes a definitive understanding of the specific characteristics associated with persistence, resourcefulness, and initiative in autonomous learning, coupled with self-efficacy beliefs that facilitate learners who can endure and sustain their learning in any setting or medium. Their research was predicated on the belief that autonomous learning behaviors can be identified and quantified through the development of items that assess the relative capacity of intentions to learn (that is, conation).

The original research focused on the development of a conceptual framework that adequately addresses these questions: What are the specific attributes of learners who exhibit initiative, resourcefulness, and persistence in learning? Does the medium or setting make a difference with regard to learner autonomy? What is the importance of developing lifelong, independent learners?

Perspectives regarding teaching and learning have seen a subtle shift over the past decade. There is a greater emphasis on the learner and on the structures and mechanisms that sustain and develop the skills and attitudes needed for the future. The shift in thinking has focused on the internal conditions that are necessary for sustained and enduring learning rather than on the external surroundings and settings.

Distance education has reinforced the emphasis on cognitive and psychological conditions that support learning as we continue to move toward anytime-anyplace learning. The online format is viewed as an alternative way to learn in a technologically driven society that focuses on time, opportunity, and convenience as critical considerations for learning endeavors. However, regardless of the medium that is provided, it is only through understanding the role of autonomy in learning that the goals of education will ultimately be accomplished.

Background of the Problem

The rapid growth in numbers of distance education courses and programs continues to have a profound impact on the ideas and beliefs that encompass teaching and learning. The use of e-mail and the Internet, coupled with Web-based coursework, has become a core method of instruction, particularly in higher education. The number of students enrolled, course offerings, and the availability of distance education as a reliable method of instruction gained tremendous momentum during the last decade.

According to Eaton (2001), the growth of online learning opportunities continues to expand the numbers of participating institutions and of students enrolling. The University of Maryland University College (UMUC) provided distance learning opportunities to over thirty countries in the world in 1999–2000 and had more than 40,000 online students; the University of Wisconsin enrolled more than 5,000 students in online courses in 1999–2000 (up from just under 2,200 in 1998–99), and the Pennsylvania State University World Campus enrolled 3,000 online students in 1999–2000—three times the enrollment of the prior year (Eaton, 2001, p. 4).

The 2000 National Student Aid Study examined the participation of undergraduate and graduate students in distance education and found that clear patterns emerged: 8 percent of undergraduates and 10 percent of graduates and first-professional students reported taking distance education courses, and those students tended to be those with family responsibilities and limited time (Sikora, 2002).

During the twelve-month 2000–01 academic year, 56 percent (2,320) of all two-year and four-year Title IV-eligible, degree-granting institutions offered distance education for any level or audience. Twelve percent of all institutions indicated that they planned to start offering distance education courses in the next three years; 31 percent did not offer any distance education courses and did not plan to offer any in the next three years. There were an estimated 3,077,000 enrollments in all distance education courses offered by two-year and four-year institutions and an estimated 2,876,000 enrollments in college-level, credit-bearing distance education courses, with 82 percent of these at the undergraduate level (Tabs, 2003). The number of student enrollments and total online certificate and degree programs is expected to continue to increase as technology becomes embedded in the foundations of our society.

According to Edelson and Pittman (2001), "The practice of distance learning is the equivalent of holding a tiger by the tail" (p. 1). Distance learning represents the most dynamic sector of adult education, particularly in the United States where World Wide Web-based electronic delivery is fast becoming the dominant mode of instruction. Although educational institutions have embraced distance education as a method of course delivery, the implications extend far beyond the institutional wall into the very essence of culture and society on a global dimension. The dynamics of change occurring in economic, social, and technological areas are compelling factors for how we interact, communicate, and learn. Distance learning and e-learning have become critical and driving growth forces in information and communication technology as new means of defining workplace environments for business and industry.

In 2000, corporations spent approximately $1.2 billion on e-learning, and this amount is expected to increase as much as $23 billion by 2005 (Commission on Technology and Adult Learning, 2001; Zenger and Uehlein, 2001). Distance and e-learning have the capacity to influence worker productivity and performance, and they directly affect the economic growth of business and industry. Skills and expertise needed for the future will require workers who are learning-oriented; distance and e-learning are the catalyst for sweeping changes in the structure of the workplace environment and the workforce. Business and industry no longer have the luxury of time to make changes in order to remain competitive and current in a global environment. The very survival of organizations depends on the rapidity in which change can occur.

Distance learning is efficient and cost-effective; however, it is a subset of the larger construct of learning. Organizations that focus on learning can effectively implement change through a culture that emphasizes learner initiative, resourcefulness, and persistence through the development of personal autonomy. Distance learning opportunities reinforce the evolution of learner control and autonomy.

Consider the challenge faced by Deloitte Consulting to train and certify fifteen thousand consultants in over three dozen countries in e-business concepts and strategies within a nine-month period in 1999. At the time, 95 percent of the training at Deloitte Consulting was classroom-based—an approach that would have cost approximately $150 million and taken over two years to implement. The result was the creation of an e-learning approach bolstered by incentives for successful completion. The plan was successfully accomplished within nine months and, more important, created an effective and cost-efficient learning organization (Gold, 2003). Learners had to be able to self-regulate their own learning.

Organizations must retool and restructure regularly and have a sustained and strategic plan for such change. The workforce is required to accommodate this emphasis by learning specific and often discrete skills independently, quickly, and in nontraditional formats. Business and industry are increasingly seeing the value of becoming a learning organization—one that focuses on a culture of learning. Distance learning and e-learning are the dominant forces in the design and delivery of organizational and employer development.

Distance education is neither a new method of educational design and delivery nor a new idea or concept. According to Jayroe (1998), distance education evolved in the early 1700s in the form of postal-delivered correspondence. The advances in distance education have seen unparalleled growth in design, delivery, and number of courses. The future possibilities appear unlimited and continue to have a profound impact on how we communicate and how we learn (Leh, 1999).

Distance education can be any form of instructional delivery in which the student and teacher are not physically in the same location. The teaching and learning is accomplished through modes that are either *asynchronous* (teaching and learning not limited by time and place) or *synchronous* (teaching and learning requiring a definitive time and specific location). According to the American Association of University Professors (1998), distance education is "the process whereby the education of a student occurs in circumstances where the educator and student are geographically separated, and the communication across the distance is accomplished by one or more forms of technology" (p. 32). Asynchronous distance education includes methods of instruction using the postal system, videocassettes or CD-ROMs, computer-based conferencing, Web-based bulletin boards, or e-mail (Leach and Walker, 2000). Synchronous distance education includes Web-based chats, Internet relay chats, multiple-user domains, satellite broadcasts, radio broadcasts, audioconferences, and two-way conferencing (Steiner, 1995). What distinguishes the two broad forms of distance education is the order of interaction between participants; one occurs immediately, the other at a time and place determined by the individual.

Learners who use distance learning do so for a variety of reasons but particularly for convenience and access and for the advantage of anytime-anyplace learning. Students can discuss the freedom of learning at 3 A.M. while in their pajamas and eating ice cream. However, many distance learning programs focus on the delivery of the program and do not place enough emphasis on the learning that is to occur. Well-designed distance learning should not be viewed as correspondence courses; the environment is the medium and not the outcome. Traditional course curricula cannot be transferred to a distance learning platform; the goals and the objectives of the course should remain constant, but the delivery must be suited to the medium. The strategies that are used in well-developed distance learning courses take account of the characteristics of the medium, and the primary delivery is through online communication.

Distance learning requires a skill-set that is not usually associated with learning. The traditional learning setting has been face-to-face, with a highly prescriptive structure and little opportunity for independence in thought, action, or learning. The focus is on the answer rather than on the application and synthesis of knowledge. Assignments are detailed with a level of specificity that leaves little opportunity for creative thought and action. Learning is instructor-centered, with the teacher or professor providing the content. Autonomy is neither encouraged nor usually even considered a component of the formal learning setting. If an essential goal of education is to produce lifelong, independent learners, then we must deliberately provide those opportunities within the traditional, formal learning setting that includes distance learning.

When asked, many adults can identify specific learning events that have occurred as a result of wanting or needing to know or learn about something (informal learning). This learning that occurred outside the traditional classroom is not usually viewed with the same regard as formal learning. The primary issue is which skills and attributes were used to find the solution or answer in this informal or "other" learning. The attributes are initiative, resourcefulness, and persistence, coupled with the motivation to learn about something of interest—the very attributes that are valued as outcomes for traditional educational programs and systems. These learning events are highly autonomous; the problem is that although institutions and systems assert that lifelong learning or independent learning is an important outcome, little is done to provide events that trigger curiosity and self-direction in learning. Distance learning provides the venue for such opportunities and can be the trigger to facilitate the development of independent, lifelong learning.

In distance learning opportunities, it is essential to recognize where the learner is in his or her autonomy development. This can often be ascertained by the questions students ask. I had an experience in an online class in adult education regarding a specific assignment, which was to engage in a self-directed learning endeavor. I was not so much interested in the specific learning as I was in the documentation of the journey. I asked students to engage in some learning that was of interest to them and to develop a PowerPoint presentation at the end of the course to document their learning process. The assignment was loosely structured but had enough guidelines to provide a framework.

In the discussion area of Blackboard, a student asked me to be more specific: How many slides should they use? How many pictures? How were they to show what they had learned? What font would look best? This exchange went on for about a week, with the student's obvious discomfort at not being told exactly what to do. My response to the student was, "I can be highly prescriptive and provide a great many specific requirements *if that is what a student needs* because, after all, it [more structure, guidance, prescription] is about the student at a specific place in his or her learning." After a few days, the student responded that he now understood what I wanted them to do, that is, be autonomous, self-directed, independent learners. The student had made a quantum leap in understanding what the possibilities could be with regard to learning capabilities.

The real purpose of education is to facilitate the learning journey and become fully autonomous in your ability to sustain and endure regardless of the medium, the location, the need. Learners can and do become directors of their own learning when they are given the following structure:

- Provide opportunities to learn about something that is of interest and value.
- Provide opportunities for learning that arouse curiosity in the learner.
- Provide learning events that are not prescriptive but fluid and flexible.
- Scaffold difficult learning so that successes can be used to build further learning.
- Provide support, not answers.
- Provide a stance that the learning journey is the real outcome.
- Provide environments that foster collaboration and collegiality.
- Empower students through opportunities for self-reflection and self-appraisal.
- Provide opportunities for mastery experiences.
- Tell students you believe in their capacity to effect change and make a difference—in other words, to enhance their self-efficacy.

The traditional approaches and frameworks surrounding educational pedagogy and methodology have emphasized the social and environmental conditions of teaching and learning. The literature on distance education is a subset of all research conducted in education and still has many facets to be explored and investigated.

According to Merisotis and Olsen (2000), although a plethora of literature on the distance education phenomenon is available, *original* research on distance education is limited. Distance education evaluation is concerned primarily with (1) student outcomes (achievement, grades, test scores), (2) attitudes of students and instructors, and (3) satisfaction of students and instructors (Walker, 2002). Research on factors that can be quantified and analyzed is important in the examination of trends and provides data for program evaluation. However, additional research into the attributes and characteristics of the learner will provide information to better structure those programs for sustained and enduring learning.

Lifelong Learning for the Twenty-First Century and Beyond

Vail (1996) asserts that "to be a human being is to be a continual learner in all of one's life" (p. xvi). Vail posits that we live and work in permanent whitewater, that is, continual learning occurs under constantly changing conditions. There is little doubt that we live in a world of the rapid obsolescence of existing knowledge. In addition, information is created and generated faster than it can be accessed. This paramount certainty has a direct and extraordinary impact on teaching and learning. The breadth and depth of information and knowledge available at the touch of a keystroke via the World Wide Web has profound implications for deciding what information and skills are important and of long-term value for the learner.

The questions that arise are these: (1) How do we create learning environments in which the learner develops the skills associated with autonomous learning (initiative, resourcefulness, and persistence), and (2) How do we create environments that support the cognitive and psychological conditions necessary for learner success and enhance lifelong learning through the development of personal learner autonomy? The research in self-directed learning has focused on external management and on the conditions that individuals exhibit in personal learning endeavors (Houle, 1961; Johnstone and Rivera, 1965; Tough, 1979). Although these variables quantify specific variables such as time, place, and duration with regard to learning, they do not explain the psychological and cognitive conditions that exist and are required for independence in learning. Theoretical and conceptual models developed by Derrick (2001), Carr (1999), and Ponton (1999) have identified specific behaviors through which to understand persistence, resourcefulness, and initiative, respectively, in autonomous learning endeavors; other research has considered the factor of self-efficacy as a reinforcement for learner autonomy (Derrick, Carr, and Ponton, forthcoming).

Understanding Autonomous Learning

Understanding the key factors and behaviors associated with an individual's proclivity to engage in lifelong learning has remained ambiguous, despite continued research and study in this area. Houle (1961) writes, "Effort to explore the reasons why some people become continuing learners has made it clear that there is no simple answer to this complex question" (p. 80). During the 1960s, research focused on how and why adults engage in learning activities. Houle (1961) focused on adults who retain alert and inquiring minds throughout the years of maturity. This work was followed by a nationwide study, undertaken by Johnstone and Rivera (1965), who determined that "self-learning" activities make up a major part of the learning being undertaken by adults in the United States. Tough (1979) found that 20 percent of adult learning was planned and organized by someone other than the learner, whereas 80 percent was self-planned and self-guided. Tough's research became the basis for numerous studies that verified the existence of self-learning and exposed the prevalence and pervasiveness of self-planned and executed learning activities. Confessore (1992) established the notion that "self-directed [autonomous] learning manifests itself in people who feel a need to learn something" (p. 3). He also asserts that success is ultimately dependent on the individual's personal desire, initiative, resourcefulness, and persistence. This foundational theory became the underpinning for the identification of the specific behaviors associated with initiative, resourcefulness, and persistence in autonomous learning.

Initiative in Autonomous Learning. Ponton (1999) defines *personal initiative* as a behavioral syndrome of five co-occurring behaviors: (1) goal-directedness, (2) action-orientation, (3) active approach to problem solving, (4) persistence in overcoming obstacles, and (5) self-startedness. Ponton's research describes the importance of establishing goals and working toward the accomplishment of those goals, the speed with which an individual transfers the intention to engage in some learning activity into action, the role of self-motivation, the ability to assume responsibility for finding solutions to barriers or obstacles that may occur in learning, and the ability to sustain action, despite the presence of obstacles.

Resourcefulness in Autonomous Learning. Carr (1999) identifies the behaviors of learner resourcefulness as anticipating future rewards of learning, prioritizing learning over other activities, choosing learning over other activities, and solving one's problems in learning. The resourceful learner is able to recognize the anticipated future value of the learning, keep the learning a priority despite other goals or obstacles, postpone activities that may be exciting or fun for the future value of the learning, and solve problems related to the learning endeavor.

Persistence in Autonomous Learning. Derrick (2001) asserts that persistence in a learning endeavor is the volitional behavior that enables the individual to sustain the effort and perseverance necessary to remain focused on the achievement of a goal, despite obstacles, distractions, and competing goals. Volition is the mediating force between intentions to learn and the behaviors needed to learn, that is, the strength of the desire or reasons for and against acting on that desire. Volitional control is the commitment to a goal and is attained by the regulation of self. Self-regulation of those enduring behaviors necessary for goal attainment is contingent on volition. The strength of the desire for acting in a particular way influences the level of volition required to self-regulate the behavior.

Autonomous learning is the process in which the learner makes an intentional decision to assume the responsibility for a learning situation.

Although the theoretical construct of autonomous learning explains the factors associated with and necessary for success for autonomous learning endeavors, it is not a sufficient explanation for understanding learners who sustain and maintain lifelong learning endeavors, either in formal situations, such as in an academic setting, or in informal or other learning settings. Learner autonomy, coupled with self-efficacy beliefs, will enhance and facilitate the understanding of enduring learners, that is, individuals who learn continually and independently in any setting or condition.

Self-Efficacy in Autonomous Learning. Self-efficacy is the belief in one's ability to organize and execute the sources of action required to manage prospective situations (Bandura, 1986). Belief in one's personal efficacy constitutes the key factor of human agency and determines the choices that are made in hopes of achieving a desired outcome. The construct of self-efficacy, coupled with the factors associated with autonomous learning (resourcefulness, initiative, persistence), should be considerations in the design of programs to enhance and facilitate enduring learners.

Self-efficacy is mediated by a person's beliefs or expectations about his or her capacity to accomplish a task or demonstrate a specific behavior. Bandura (1997) asserts that these expectations determine whether or not a certain behavior or performance will be attempted, the amount of effort the individual will contribute to the behavior, and how long the behavior will be sustained when obstacles are encountered.

Figure 1.1 provides a model for understanding the relationship between motivation, self-efficacy, and the factors associated with learner autonomy.

In any learning event, it is important to structure opportunities for learning that build on prior successes and establish new and more challenging goals for the future. The motivation to engage in any learning event is predicated on whether one believes learning is possible and on what one

Figure 1.1. Relationship of Motivation, Self-Efficacy, and Autonomous Learning

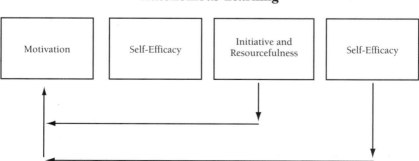

Source: Derrick, Carr, and Ponton, forthcoming. Used by permission.

believes about his or her ability to be successful with regard to the outcomes of that learning behavior. A strong entering motivation is not likely to be sustainable if success seems unlikely. As individuals experience success in learning, their sense of efficacy is enhanced to engage in additional learning of a more difficult nature, provided success is attributed to personal capability. As people become better equipped through positive learning experiences that move them toward being a fully autonomous learner, their efficacy beliefs are reinforced and enhanced.

Bandura (1997) identifies four sources of efficacy information: (1) performance accomplishments, (2) vicarious learning, (3) verbal persuasion, and (4) physical or affective status. Performance accomplishments in an online format should allow for student success through goal or task accomplishment of more difficult tasks and assignments. Learners are not successful in every assignment or task; however, temporary obstacles should not become permanent barriers to success but should be viewed as opportunities to learn.

Beliefs about abilities are acquired through observation and interpretation; the learner reflects on past experiences and makes meaning in new situations. Observational experiences allow for learner self-reflection and the anticipation of new experiences.

Beliefs about the self are influenced by the messages conveyed by others. Verbal persuasion can be used to encourage students' self-efficacy and career aspirations through acquisition of the terminal degree. Stress and anxiety have a negative impact on self-efficacy as well as learning; a supportive and encouraging environment enhances and facilitates learning.

Enduring Learners

The exercise of human agency through individuals' personal beliefs in their capacity and ability to produce a desired change by their actions through quadratic reciprocity of learner autonomy and self-efficacy beliefs will produce learners who are successful in formal and in other learning endeavors. These four factors (self-efficacy, initiative, resourcefulness, and persistence) are reciprocal processes that ultimately determine the state of the learner. The model of quadratic reciprocity (Figure 1.2) explains how these factors are connected, producing a cohesive theory that adequately explains the concept of the enduring learner. The development of the attributes associated with learner autonomy, coupled with self-efficacy beliefs, produces learners who view any learning endeavor with certainty and affirmation.

Four factors determine the state of the learner: (1) initiative, (2) resourcefulness, (3) persistence, and (4) the coupling of persistence and self-efficacy. These four factors are co-occurring and bidirectional in nature, that is, they are reciprocal processes. This conceptual model explains how and what forces are necessary to produce an enduring learner.

Figure 1.2. Model of Quadratic Reciprocity

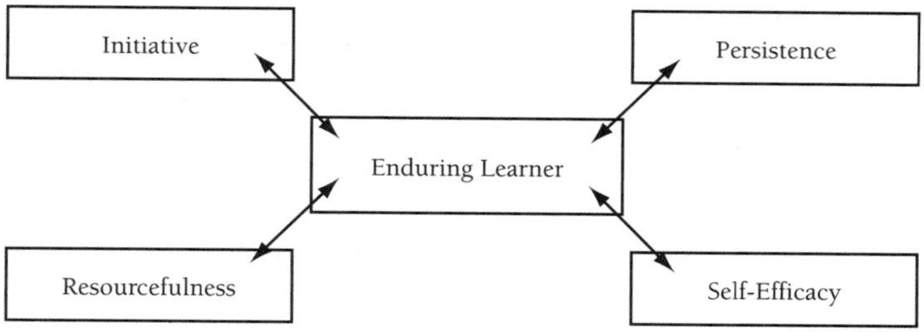

Source: Derrick, Carr, and Ponton, forthcoming. Used by permission.

Enduring learners continue to learn throughout life and view learning as the never-ending journey of self-fulfillment and self-satisfaction. These learners have a strong sense of efficacy with regard to their individual capacity to learn, brought about through prior experiences and events in learning in any setting or condition.

Changing Paradigms for Teaching and Learning

It is important to distinguish between theories of teaching and theories of learning. Rogers (1969) asserts:

> Teaching, in my estimation, is a vastly over-rated function. Having made such a statement, I scurry to the dictionary to see if I really mean what I say. Teaching means "to instruct." Personally, I am not much interested in instructing another in what he should know or think. "To impact knowledge or skill." My reaction is, why not be more efficient, using a book or programmed learning? "To make to know." Here my hackles rise. I have no wish to make anyone know something. "To show, guide, direct." As I see it, too many people have been shown, guided, directed. So I come to the conclusion that I do mean what I said. Teaching is, for me, a relatively unimportant and vastly overvalued activity (p. 103).

Rogers goes on to explain that his view of teaching and the imparting of knowledge makes sense in an unchanging environment, which is why it has been an unquestioned function for centuries. "But, if there is one truth about modern man, it is that he lives in an environment that is constantly changing," and therefore the aim of education must be on the facilitation of learning (pp. 104–105).

The traditional learning setting has changed with distance learning options. This is evident when one *teaches* in this environment. I use this term loosely because my goal is to facilitate learners from a relatively dependent view regarding their capacity for autonomous learning to one of comparative independence.

Experience with postgraduate students in an online program reveals their academic ability for success; this is evident in an examination of their undergraduate and graduate records. What the students lack are the skills for lifelong, independent learning—skills that are not bound to a professor or teacher or by textbooks and curriculum. The skills and behaviors needed for success require competence in areas that reside in the psychological dimensions of the learner. Achievement is not contingent on the kinds of behaviors that have historically been associated with success in learning; most students have little experience in environments that expect and demand independent learner endeavors. This often causes a great deal of cognitive discomfort as students become fully autonomous in their learning.

It is interesting to note that learners do not equate the skills used in *other* learning (those associated with independent activities outside traditional classrooms in which the student takes the initiative to learn something, is resourceful in that learning, and is persistent until a satisfactory sense of accomplishment is achieved) with the skills that are also necessary in any learning endeavor and in any setting, but particularly learning associated with formal learning and education. The opportunity to enhance the behaviors associated with autonomous learning complements the distance learning setting with appropriate learning situations.

The emphasis on the structures and mechanisms of educational practice has been supplanted by the effort to understand the attributes and behaviors of the learner and, more important, to determine how to facilitate and enhance the behaviors and attributes needed for successful learning, regardless of the medium or the setting. Contemporary beliefs regarding teaching and learning place a greater emphasis on understanding the internal conditions necessary for successful learning and less emphasis on the external structures and systems.

According to Schunk and Zimmerman (1994), "Educators have moved away from explanations of learning and performance that stress learners' abilities and responses to environmental stimuli . . . to concern with students' attempts to manage their achievement efforts through activities that influence the instigation, direction and persistence of those efforts" (p. ix).

An essential understanding of the psychological and cognitive conditions associated with sustained and enduring learning will support learners in any medium or any setting. Once learners are able to understand their own capacities for learning—any learning—they are fundamentally changed with regard to their personal view of their capabilities and competence. The learning reinforces beliefs and efficacious behaviors for lifelong and sustained learning.

References

American Association of University Professors, Subcommittee on Distance Learning. "Distance Learning." *Academe,* May-June 1998, *84*(3), 30–38.

Bandura, A. *Social Foundations of Thought and Action: A Social Cognitive Theory.* Englewood Cliffs, N.J.: Prentice Hall, 1986.

Bandura, A. *Self-Efficacy: The Exercise of Control.* New York: Freeman, 1997.

Carr, P. B. "The Measurement of Resourcefulness Intentions in the Adult Autonomous Learner." Doctoral dissertation, The George Washington University, *Dissertation Abstracts International,* 1999, *60,* 3849.

Commission on Technology and Adult Learning. *A Vision of E-Learning for America's Workforce.* Alexandria, Va.: American Society for Training and Development, and Washington, D.C.: National Governors' Association. Retrieved Mar. 23, 2003, from http://nga.org/cda/files/ELEARNINGREPORT.pdf, 2001.

Confessore, G. J. "An Introduction to the Study of Self-Directed Learning." In G. J. Confessore and S. J. Confessore (eds.), *Guideposts to Self-Directed Learning: Expert Commentary on Essential Concepts.* King of Prussia, Penn.: Organization Design and Development, 1992.

Derrick, M. G. "The Measurement of an Adult's Intention to Exhibit Persistence in Autonomous Learning." Doctoral dissertation, The George Washington University, *Dissertation Abstracts International,* 2001, *62/05,* 2533.

Derrick, M. G., Carr, P. B., and Ponton, M. K. "Enhancing and Facilitating Self-Efficacious Behaviors in Distance Learning Environments." Forthcoming.

Eaton, J. S. "Distance Learning; Academic and Political Challenges for Higher Education Accreditation." Council for Higher Education Accreditation (CHEA Monograph Series no. 1, 2001). Retrieved from http://www.chea.org/Research/distance-learning/chea_dis_learning.pdf, 2001.

Edelson, P. J., and Pittman, V. V. "E-Learning in the United States: New Directions and Opportunities for University Continuing Education." *Global E-Journal of Open, Flexible and Distance Education,* 2001, *1*(1), 71–73.

Gold, M. "Enterprise E-Learning." *Learning Circuits: ASTD's Online Magazine.* Retrieved from http://www.learningcircuits.org, 2003.

Houle, C. O. *The Inquiring Mind: A Study of the Adult Learner Who Continues to Participate to Learn.* Madison: University of Wisconsin Press, 1961.

Jayroe, L. J. "The Evolution of Distance Education: Impact and Implications for the 21st Century Educator" (Human Anatomy and Physiology Society Web site). Retrieved from http://www.hapsweb.org/Library/Jayroe_HAPS98_presentation/sld015.htm, 1998.

Johnstone, J.W.C., and Rivera, R. J. *Volunteers for Learning.* Hawthorne, N.Y.: Aldine de Gruyter, 1965.

Leach, K., and Walker, S. "Internet-Based Distance Education: Barriers, Models, and New Research." In *Proceedings of WebNet World Conference on the World Wide Web and the Internet 2000,* Oct. 30–Nov. 4, 2000. Charlottesville, Va.: Association for the Advancement of Computing in Education, 2000.

Leh, A. "Computer-Mediated Communication and Foreign Language Learning Via Telecommunication Technology." In B. Collis and R. Oliver (eds.), *Proceedings of Ed-Media 1999: World Conference on Educational Multimedia, Hypermedia, and Telecommunications,* Seattle, June 19–24, 1999. Charlottesville, Va.: Association for the Advancement of Computing in Education, 1999.

Merisotis, J. P., and Olsen, J. K. "The 'Effectiveness Debate': What We Know About the Quality of Distance Learning in the U.S." *TechKnowLogia,* 2000, *2*(1), 42–44.

Ponton, M. K. "The Measurement of an Adult's Intention to Exhibit Personal Initiative in Autonomous Learning." Doctoral dissertation, The George Washington University, *Dissertation Abstracts International,* 1999, *60,* 3933.

Rogers, C. R. *Freedom to Learn*. Columbus, Ohio: Merrill, 1969.

Schunk, D. H., and Zimmerman, B. J. *Self-Regulation of Learning and Performance*. Hillsdale, N.J.: Erlbaum, 1994.

Sikora, A. C. "A Profile of Participation in Distance Education: 1999–2000." NCES (National Center for Education Statistics). Available from http://nces.ed.gov/pubsearch/pubsinfo.asp?pubid=20033154, 2002.

Steiner, V. "What Is Distance Education?" *Distance Learning Resource Network*. Retrieved Mar. 23, 2003, from http://www.dlrn.org/library/dlwhatis.html, 1995.

Tabs, E. D. "Distance Education at Degree Granting Post-Secondary Institutions: 2000–2001" (National Center for Educational Statistics). Retrieved from http://nces.ed.gov/pubs2003/2003017.pdf, July 20, 2003.

Tough, A. *The Adult's Learning Project*. San Diego: University Associates, 1979.

Vail, P. *Learning As a Way of Being*. San Francisco: Jossey-Bass, 1996.

Walker, S. "Evaluation, Description and Effects of Distance Education Learning Environments in Higher Education." Paper presented at the 9th Annual International Distance Education Conference, Austin, Tex., Jan. 22–25, 2002. Retrieved from http://www.centerfordistancelearning, Mar. 23, 2003.

Zenger, J., and Uehlein, C. "Why Blended Will Win." *T & D*, Aug. 2001, 55(8), 54–60.

M. GAIL DERRICK is an associate professor in the School of Education at Regent University, Virginia Beach, Virginia.

2

Effective online education is a blend of pedagogy, technology, and organizational support. For meaningful online learning experiences, prospective online learners should evaluate the strengths of these three elements and play an active role in exploring the increased interaction opportunity that online learning provides.

In Search of Meaningful Online Learning Experiences

Seung-won Yoon

In writing this chapter, I have the following individuals in mind: online education course instructors, technical support teams, administrators, policymakers, and prospective online learners. I find it does a disservice to ignore any of these, because online students' learning experiences are largely shaped by their interactions with the course materials, technological interfaces, their peers, and all these key players in a technology-mediated environment. Therefore, without looking at the various aspects of products, services, and interactions that online learning provides, the learning outcome of online education cannot be fairly judged.

Viewing online learning as an alternative form to the traditional classroom learning, where technology-mediated interactions try to emulate face-to-face interactions, is a common mistake in comparing the two learning environments. Online learning environments, especially technology-mediated interactions, are relatively new and are different from time- and place-dependent face-to-face interactions. The growth and prevalence of online learning in the knowledge economy call for asking how to enhance the online students' learning experiences. This chapter presents a framework that views successful online learning experiences resulting from the blend of pedagogy, technology, and organizational support and highlights the active role expected of prospective online learners.

Comparison of Educational Settings

Although technological advances are blurring the distinction between traditional and online education settings, differences still abound between them. It is particularly helpful to compare the two settings for adult learners who are considering online education as the primary learning path.

Definitions. In a traditional education setting, people go to a physical location and attend an instructor- or a trainer-led course. The term *classroom instruction* is homogeneously used to represent such an instructional and learning arrangement.

In contrast, several terms are used to refer to instruction and learning delivered via online methodologies. *Online learning, virtual learning, Web-based learning, technology-based learning, e-learning, network-based learning,* and *computer-based learning* emphasize the learning technology and tools used. *Distance education* and *distributed learning* focus on the difference in location between a learner and a teacher, or, in many cases, among the learners. *Asynchronous learning* reflects the reliance on time-delayed communication and its time flexibility. Sometimes, a learning approach such as a *guided individual study* is used to describe this nontraditional learning environment. Among these terms, *e-learning* is most widely used in corporate settings and is defined as *the delivery of content via all electronic media* (Urdan and Weggen, 2000).

Distance education is a term that has been widely used in educational settings; the term highlights the media used and the intent to reach nontraditional students by overcoming geographical distance (McIsaac and Gunawardena, 1996). *Online education* is becoming a popular term to refer to learning via the Internet and on networked computers, or intranets. Harasim (1989) points out that the traditional definition of distance education lacks the social and collaborative nature of the learning environment facilitated by computer-mediated communication and claims that "online education opens unprecedented opportunities for educational interactivity" (p. 42). Although *e-learning* is most widely used in a corporate training context, postsecondary institutions (whose market was about four times larger than that of corporate training in 2002), sporadically use this term. I use *online education* in this chapter to incorporate both e-learning and distance education, while acknowledging the common use of each term in the two different adult learning settings.

Aims. Classroom-based instruction aims to foster learning via interaction between a student and the instructor, peers, and instructional materials. This has been the golden rule of learning and is the method of instructional delivery most familiar to adult learners. This medium is effective in that clarification of the learners' questions and needs can be immediate during the presence of the instructor and peers. When it comes to the quality of classroom instruction, we understand that there is nothing inherently good about this learning arrangement.

Comparison of Methods. For meaningful learning experiences to occur, learning should emerge from students' interactions with meaningful contents, the course instructor, and peers. This learning arrangement has two major shortcomings when serving busy adult learners. First, it is mostly time- and place-dependent. Most classes are held during work hours, thus it is not the most effective in serving adult learners' needs for balancing work and continuous learning (Harasim, 1989). It is also the case that classroom instruction tends to be more expensive than online learning, especially when workers' lost opportunity costs are taken into account. Viewing online education as an alternative choice for learning due to the inaccessibility of the traditional classroom blindfolds prospective online learners to an exploration of the different types of interactions that online education fosters.

The amount of class time available to each participant is greater in online education than in traditional learning environments (Harasim, 1989). Online education allows for more frequent interactions and collaborations with peers and experts via networked communication. Digital interactions are superior to analogue interactions, or face-to-face interactions. Interactions occurring online can be stored, retrieved, and disseminated anytime and anywhere.

This storage-and-retrieval dimension is still new and awaits greater exploration. For example, synchronous group text chat can create an interactive environment in which multiple individuals from different locations can discuss a topic, share ideas, and form group consensuses. This communication mode can foster a nonthreatening communication environment and equal participation from discussants. Some software allows integrating graphics, remote contents, and audio or video to further incorporate different human senses into the communication environment. After the session, the interaction can be archived onto a server and retrieved or disseminated later.

In contrast, face-to-face interactions are time- and place-dependent and are perishable. The expanded dimension of online interaction becomes beneficial through the addition of sound pedagogy and organizational support. In order for appropriate communication and dissemination to happen, more preparation and better coordination between discussion participants and system-support individuals are required than what is found in traditional classroom learning methodologies. Technologies can be used in a creative manner to facilitate more frequent information exchanges before, during, or after the chat session, but systemic technology support from an organization is also required. As illustrated, effectively coordinated online education can create a more responsive, time- and place-flexible, and resourceful learning environment.

Prevalence of Online Education

With its greater power to reach wider audiences in a rapid and cost-effective manner, digitalization is driving product innovation, quality improvement, workflow change, global communication, and new types of business transactions. The Internet has reached the quarter of the U.S. population within the shortest amount of time among all electronic, telecommunications, and transportation products. The growth and adoption of the Internet are expected to continue, as common activities such as reading, hearing, watching, and talking are converging on the Internet and networked devices (Penzias, 1995). These changes have created a demand for adult learners to continuously learn and update skills and knowledge. Corporations and postsecondary institutions are vigorously embracing technologies in order to meet adult learners' continual learning needs.

According to the American Society for Training and Development (ASTD) 2003 Industry Report, the percentage of learning delivered via technologies for corporate training increased from 8.4 percent to 10.5 percent in 2001, whereas the percentage of total training time via the classroom declined from 79.1 to 77.1 percent. Workers' (aged twenty-five or older) use of the Internet and e-mail has seen a dramatic increase to 41.7 percent in 2001, up from 26.1 percent in 2000. A study conducted by the Department of Commerce (2002) supported this finding of increased use of the Internet; 50.5 percent of U.S. households had Internet access at home. Of this number, 76.8 percent said that someone in the household was also using the Internet at work.

A report from the National Center for Education Statistics (1999) also indicates that distance education has seen a dramatic increase of 1,195 programs in postsecondary institutions from 1995 to 1998, and the authors expect that pattern to continue. The 1998 survey from NCES found that 1,680 institutions offered a total of about 54,000 online education courses in 1998, with 1.6 million students enrolled. Certificate programs grew from 170 to 330 during the same period. This supports the observation that online learning is becoming a major learning tool for adult learners. The trend is unlikely to decline, as the benefit potentials of online learning, such as saving training costs, increasing access, reaching new audiences, providing timely information, and enhancing instructional delivery methods, are substantial.

Online Education as a Blend of Pedagogy, Technology, and Organizational Support

Innovations and changes in adult learning go beyond the technological innovations of online learning (Collis and Davies, 1995). When it comes to selecting an online education program, adult learners ask the following two questions most frequently: (1) What is in it for me? and (2) Will this work for me? However, these two questions hardly lead them to explore and examine various issues that critically affect their future learning experiences.

According to Collis and Davies (1995), effective online education for adult learners is the result of a blend of technology, pedagogy, organization, strategy, and vision. I find this statement to be true. This is a practical conceptual framework that helps all key players of online education—learners, course instructors, policymakers, administrators, and technology development or support staff members—examine issues that affect online students' learning experiences.

The last three elements (organization, strategy, and vision) can be nicely captured by organizational support. Literature on distance education has identified institutional support, interaction with faculty, feedback quality, meaningful contents, course structure, student support, faculty support, and evaluation and assessment as crucial for successful online education (Phipps and Merisotis, 2000). The blend of technology, pedagogy, and organizational support aligns with the research findings.

The following section discusses which issues are in need of further examination within each category to enhance online students' meaningful learning experiences.

Pedagogy. Often not clearly specified in advertisements are the instructional and learning approaches a program emphasizes or the technological and social infrastructure of the online education system's ability to assist in achieving the learning goals. It is easy to state learning approaches and technologies that contradict the espoused learning goals. For example, there is a mismatch between the design of online learning and pedagogy used when a program states that learning is more meaningful and effective through applications and group work with others of similar interests but implements a self-paced learning design without collaboration opportunities. This happens frequently in materials that follow a traditional lecture format but are put directly into Web-based instruction without adjustments being made to include activities and assignments.

Examining where, when, and how different types of interactions are to be managed for the target audience in a consistent manner is the first thing needing clarification. Moore (1989) identifies three types of interactions essential in distance education: (1) learner-instructor, (2) learner-content, and (3) learner-learner interaction. Added to these three interaction dimensions, today's Internet-based online education can accommodate the learners' real-world knowledge interaction by fostering students' interactions and collaboration with remote resources such as field experts and online professional communities. An increase in the interaction dimension, with greater time and place flexibility under less social presence in a technology-mediated communication environment, calls for finding a close fit between espoused learning approaches and the interaction types that a program implements.

The strengths of pedagogy can be evaluated through several sources. Some online programs provide more than one medium type for the same instructional contents (for example, slides, transcripts, and prerecorded audio) by way of addressing different learning styles. This is an effort to increase the effectiveness of the learner-content interaction. Some programs incorporate synchronous hours for students to engage in group work to improve the learner-learner interaction or clarify questions with the instructor to enhance the learner-instructor interaction. The learner-instructor interaction can also flourish through various feedback mechanisms such as office hours managed by a phone line or an instant-messenger tool. The learner–real-world knowledge interaction can be enhanced through examples, for example, by reading case studies or interacting with a leading expert. For students' meaningful online learning experiences, a single type or a combination of differing types of interaction must take place and be consistently managed in online learning.

More interaction dimensions do not necessarily mean an increase in cost for online education providers. Studies report that the initial development cost for online education is greater than that of equivalent traditional instruction, but benefits of online learning, such as the ability to recycle content, have convenient access and timely updates on content, and the capacity to reach larger audiences than with traditional methodologies can result in a greater return on investment (ROI) (Urdan and Weggen, 2000).

Technology. A variety of technologies and tools (such as print, prerecorded video and audio, discussion groups, live virtual classes, text-based chat, simulations, online references, streamed video and audio, e-mail, and learning-management systems) are all available for use in today's online education. Due to the variety of technologies and tools, grasping all technological experiences on the part of learners is a significant challenge. Students' interaction with technologies has been cited as one of the critical dimensions of online interaction because students' interaction with instructional contents, peers, the course instructor, and the administrative and technical support staff members are managed through this interaction dimension (Hillman, Willis, and Gunawardena, 1994).

Technologies are implemented to create an interactive online environment to generate communication, presentations, simulations, and demonstrations. Prospective online learners should not make a selection decision solely based on an advertisement claim that they will work with cutting-edge technologies throughout the course. They are only good as long as such technologies facilitate students' interactions, are easy to use, and are reliable. Providing a reliable system and supportive technical troubleshooting are two of the twenty-four quality benchmarks in online learning defined by the Institute for Higher Education Policy (2000).

Technologies should be examined specifically regarding how interactions and coordination will be facilitated by the technologies. The four-square map of groupware options (see Figure 2.1) provides a convenient way to understand various technologies used in online education. Instead of examining technology as an isolated tool, this map describes various media technologies according to the configuration of time and place that challenge many work groups.

Same-time and same-place arrangements imply face-to-face meetings. Same-time and different-place technologies include synchronous electronic meetings such as a real-time text chat, audio- or videoconferencing tools,

Figure 2.1. The Four-Square Map of Groupware Options

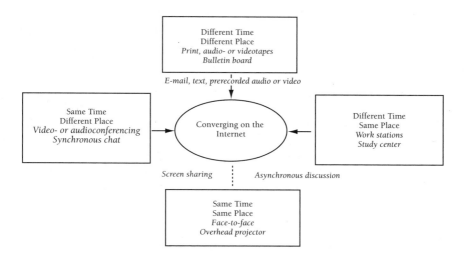

Source: Adapted from R. Johansen and others, 1991. Used by permission.

and a shared electronic white board. These tools are implemented to simulate face-to-face group meetings. Different-time and same-place technologies include shared desktop computers and bulletin or message boards. Different-time and different-place technologies include e-mail, voicemail, and Web pages. In today's online education, different tools used for these time-and-place configurations are converging on the Internet via networked devices with their capacity to incorporate text, graphics, audio, and video.

Prospective online learners can obtain information about technologies used in a program from a Web site that showcases or gives a tutorial about technologies used in the program. Most online education programs also provide technical support contact information about where further information about technological needs and experiences can be explored. Online education programs that take into account the importance of the interaction-facilitating roles that technology provides are continually working to improve students' technological experiences and minimize undue technological failures. The four-square map clarifies whether implemented technologies foster the types of interactions students look for and online programs aim to deliver.

For instance, if a program says that learning is most beneficial from collaboration and group work, and it only provides static Web pages and one-way instructional contents such as text and prerecorded audio and video, there is a poor match between the technologies being used and the pedagogy being claimed. When a program claims that stable technologies are a must but report frequent system failures, do not use back-up systems, or provide any technical emergency protocol during the downtime, the quality of coordination between different resources at the program level needs to be questioned.

Adult learners understand that technologies change rapidly. When new technologies are implemented or changes are made to the current system, time must be dedicated to test and try the system so that technological experiences become stable before the learners interact with them. Organizations that harness the power of digital technologies by responding to and anticipating the needs of customers continue to gain more business (Negroponte, 1995). When an online education program fails to deliver the products and services adult learners need, it can only lose them to another program that delivers on its promises.

Organizational Support. Students' meaningful learning experiences through interactive learning environments and reliable technology are sustainable only when there is an organization with clear vision, strategies, and support for online education. Among the factors identified through the literature, institutional support, faculty support, and assessment and evaluation are particularly relevant to this issue.

Maintaining and refining an effective online program requires substantial human and financial resources. In order to sustain and promote effective online teaching and learning, organizations should provide various services for the learners and the course instructors. Learner support includes access to library and learning resources, facilities, administrative assistance with admission, registration, and textbook information, along with technical support during the course. Support for the course instructor includes budgetary and policy issues such as rewards and compensation, curriculum development, copyright of course materials and other intellectual property, and evaluation and assessment tools. Course structure and design, development, delivery, and assessment should not be left solely to the course instructor because doing so creates a high risk of structural inconsistencies among different courses.

In evaluating the quality of online education, several professional associations such as the Institute for Higher Education Policy (2000), North Central Association Commission on Institutions of Higher Education (2000), and American Council on Education (2000) identify institutional support (for example, student support, faculty support, evaluation and assessment, and curriculum development support), as crucial for meeting quality standards in distance education. Quality standards for e-learning in corporate settings have been mostly directed at the individual course level (E-Learning Competency Center, 2002) and at enhancing interoperability among different courseware tools. Institutional support unique to the corporate training setting has included sponsorship of e-learning from the top management and the fostering of a cooperative work relationship between the human resource department and the information technology department (American Society for Training and Development, 2003).

Visionary, Strategic, and Supportive Corporations. In the knowledge economy, workers need to process more information in a shorter amount of time and continue to update knowledge about changing work processes, regulations, and transactional laws. As a result, companies need to deliver knowledge and update skills rapidly and efficiently whenever and wherever possible (Urdan and Weggen, 2000).

Visionary companies bring learning to people. They understand that trained employees actively participate in product innovations and quality improvement. They also view e-learning as a strategic tool to maximize human capital in the knowledge economy. They implement technologies to distinguish their products and services from those of their competitors.

Large corporations provide online courses ranging from technical to managerial subject matter when classroom instruction is not cost-effective for training large numbers of employees in the shortest amount of time. Sometimes, geographical dispersion makes on-site training less attractive due to the high costs of traveling and lodging. In such circumstances, online education is a strategic tool in reducing training costs and allowing for the training of large numbers of employees at any given time. Organizational support for e-learning can be found from examples such as employees' direct access to online courses and tuition support when they work toward an online degree program at a postsecondary institute. This not only improves the retention of active employees but provides the firm with an effective recruiting tool to attract highly motivated and learning-oriented individuals.

Access to online education is also given to suppliers, contractors, and consumers on an as-needed basis to enhance the transactional relationship. Course lengths range from several months to brief, just-in-time job aid. Some companies provide a searchable reference library and online books. Wide access to a networked desktop computer at work and home makes online education a convenient and cost-effective learning tool.

Visionary, Strategic, and Supportive Higher Education Institutes. Proponents of online learning in higher education settings embrace it for the increased educational opportunities and improvement of learning and instruction that online methodologies provide. The digest of education statistics from NCES (2002) reports that the enrollment of students who are twenty-five or older is expected to increase at 9 percent between 2000 and 2010. According to Urdan and Weggen (2000), traditional students between the age of eighteen and twenty-two make up less than 20 percent of all students in higher education. Visionary higher education institutes see diverse segments of adult learners they can further reach via online education.

Addressing the different populations of adult learners not only improves equity needs but better prepares the future workforce. Working professionals who want to advance their careers by taking courses online, executives who travel frequently but want to earn an advanced degree, and parents who want to finish their undergraduate work without giving up their work and family responsibilities are all potential learners who can benefit from online education.

For many universities and community colleges, technology frequently appears on the president's list of institutional achievements. Comprehensive support for student services, faculty development and training, curriculum development, evaluation, and assessment, and technologies often go beyond the resources of one institution; thus institutions often seek accreditation, partnerships between vendors, and cooperation with other universities. Sometimes, alliances between institutions from different (or the same) states are formed to improve the learner segments they serve. Adult learners in the knowledge economy expect the time, place, and pace of education to be convenient to the learner and expect that education will enhance their employment and income prospects.

Potential Challenges

Muilenburg and Berge (2001) identify ineffective administrative structure, organizational change, lack of technical expertise, poor social interaction and quality, lack of faculty compensation and time, threat of technology, legal issues, evaluation effectiveness, student access, and student-support services as common barriers to successful distance education. Regardless of different online learning settings, students' meaningful learning experiences come from an effective online education program in which course instructors, instructional designers, learners, system developers, technical support staff members, managers, and administrators closely collaborate to use technologies for fostering active and interactive learning environments.

The blend of pedagogy, technology, and organizational support will be negatively affected not only by a poor alignment between the key players but by any failure of any one key party. Therefore, one party should see its role as a facilitator of the entire online education program system, as well as a feedback mechanism to enhance the products and services produced by another party. For example, course instructors are pedagogically challenged to create and sustain social presence in online learning for adult learners who have diverse learning styles but commonly demand feedback and clarification. Meeting the demands will only be sustainable when technical support teams and the institution provide assistance with course development and delivery methods.

On the part of the organization, most informative feedback about the quality of online education can be obtained from the front-end users such as the course instructor and the learners. They can provide human, financial, and technological supports for online education but need to interact with the users to diagnose the quality of students' learning experiences. Finally, the learners must understand that they need to stay responsible and active throughout the program in order to maximize the potential benefits of online learning.

The expanded dimension of online learning can also result in a more passive learning environment, where fewer initiatives and responsive interactions tend to result in suboptimal learning experiences. Monitoring and facilitating learner interactions are more time-consuming activities on the part of the course instructor, thus finding a way to alleviate the burden and enhance the learning experiences remains a challenge. Technological support to trace learner participation or peer evaluation is one of many possibilities that can be explored and supported. Fortunately, online education has multiple indicators and key players that, combined, can explore new ways to provide feedback and enhance students' learning experiences.

Expected Learner Roles

Lifelong learning, just-in-time learning, experiential learning, self-directed learning, and collaborative learning have become crucial for adult learners in the knowledge economy. Online education provides a practical, convenient, and economical opportunity for adult learners who are unable to take advantage of residential educational opportunities. As in the traditional classroom, online learners' experiences are largely shaped by their interaction with various sources, but the types of interactions fostered in an online environment are still new and call for greater exploration and coordination.

Conclusion

This chapter reviewed the strengths and challenges of online education and discussed how effective online education is a blend of pedagogy, technology, and organizational support. As has been described, an effectively coordinated online education program is able to foster meaningful learning experiences through unprecedented opportunities for educational interactivity.

As key players in online education, the learners are at the forefront of exploring and experiencing new educational interactivity. As end users of a learning system, they are in a good position to evaluate whether an online program has strengths in pedagogy, technology, and organizational support and to determine whether a strong blend exists. They should not be passive recipients of online education. Instead, they need to be actively involved in the process of designing and executing changes to provide feedback to online education providers and improve their online learning experiences. Online learning is a powerful and effective tool for adult learners who want to learn by maximizing the use of expanded interaction opportunities in their work and personal environments.

References

American Council on Education. *Developing a Distance Education Policy for 21st Century Learning,* 2000. Retrieved from http://www.acenet.edu/washington/distance_ed/ 2000/03march/distance_ed.html, Mar. 26, 2003.

American Society for Training and Development. *ASTD Roadmap for E-learning.* 2003. Retrieved from http://www.astd.org/virtual_community/Comm_elrng_rdmap/roadmap.html, Mar. 22, 2003.

Collis, B., and Davies, G. *Innovative Adult Learning with Innovative Technologies.* New York: Elsevier, 1995.

E-learning Competency Center. *Quality Criteria for E-Learning Courseware,* 2002. Retrieved from http://www.ecc.org.sg/cocoon/ecc/website/qualitycriteria2.pdf, Apr. 4, 2002.

Harasim, L. "Online Education: A New Domain." In R. Mason and A. R. Kaye (eds.), *Mindweave: Communication, Computers and Distance Education.* Oxford: Pergamon Press, 1989.

Hillman, D. C., Willis, D. J., and Gunawardena, C. N. "Learner-Interface Interaction in Distance Education: An Extension of Contemporary Models and Strategies for Practitioners." *The American Journal of Distance Education,* 1994, 8(2), 30–42.

Institute for Higher Education Policy. *Quality on the Line: Benchmarks for Success in Internet-Based Distance Education.* Washington, D.C.: Institute for Higher Education Policy, 2000. Retrieved from http://www.ihep.com/Pubs/PDF/Quality.pdf, Mar. 3, 2003.

Johansen, R., Martin, A., Mittman, R., and Saffo, P. *Leading Business Teams: How Teams Can Use Technology and Group Process Tools to Enhance Performance.* Reading, Mass.: Addison-Wesley, 1991.

McIsaac, M. S., and Gunawardena, C. N. "Distance Education." In D. H. Jonassen (ed.), *Handbook of Research for Educational Communications and Technology* (Association for Educational Communications and Technology). New York: Simon & Schuster, 1996.

Moore, M. G. "Three Types of Interaction." *The American Journal of Distance Education,* 1989, 3(2), 1–6.

Muilenburg, L. Y., and Berge, Z. L. "Barriers to Distance Education: A Factor-Analytic Study." *The American Journal of Distance Education,* 2001, 15(2), 7–22.

National Center for Education Statistics. *Distance Education at Postsecondary Education Institutions: 1997–98* (NCES Report no. 2000–013). Washington, D.C.: U.S. Department of Education, 1999.

Negroponte, N. *Being Digital.* London: Hodder & Stoughton, 1995.

North Central Association. *Guidelines for Distance Education.* Chicago: North Central Association Commission on Institutions of Higher Education, 2000. Retrieved from http://www.ncacihe.org/resources/guidelines/gdistance.html, Apr. 9, 2003.

Penzias, A. "Revolution." In A. Penzias, *Harmony: Business, Technology, and Life after Paperwork.* New York: Harper Business, 1995.

Phipps, R., and Merisotis, J. "Quality on the Line: Benchmarks for Success in Internet-Based Education." Washington, D.C.: Institute for Higher Education Policy, 2000. Retrieved Mar. 3, 2003, from http://www.ihep.com/Pubs/PDF/Quality.pdf.

Urdan, T., and Weggen, C. *Corporate E-Learning: Exploring a New Frontier.* W. R. Hambrecht, 2000.

U.S. Department of Commerce. *A Nation Online: How Americans Are Expanding Their Use of the Internet,* 2002. Retrieved from the U.S. Department of Commerce, National Telecommunications and Information Administration Web site: http://www.ntia.doc.gov/ntiahome/dn/index.html, Mar. 22, 2003.

SEUNG-WON YOON is an assistant professor in the Department of Instructional Technology and Telecommunications at Western Illinois University, Macomb.

3

*The rapid growth of Web-based instruction has raised
many questions about the quality of online courses. This
chapter presents a conceptual framework that can guide
the development of online courses by providing a holistic
perspective on online teaching and learning. Examples of
instructional strategies that fit the framework are
described.*

An Instructional Strategy Framework for Online Learning Environments

Scott D. Johnson, Steven R. Aragon

Distance education is an instructional delivery system that allows students to participate in an educational opportunity without being physically present in the same location as the instructor. Although print-based correspondence study is the traditional method of distance education, more contemporary approaches rely heavily on various forms of instructional technology (Garrison, 1987).

The reason for much of the growth in distance education programs in recent years is the development of the Internet and improvement of technologies that support online learning environments. For example, among higher education institutions offering distance education, use of two-way interactive video and one-way prerecorded video was essentially the same in 1997–98 as in 1995, whereas the use of asynchronous Internet-based technologies nearly tripled in that same time period (Lewis, Snow, Farris, Levin, and Greene, 1999), and 88 percent of higher education institutions now plan to use Internet courses as their primary mode of instructional delivery for distance education (Waits, Lewis, and Greene, 2003). This change is not new to the distance education community, which has seen technology-based educational innovations come and go with much fanfare. The instructional films of the 1940s were expected to radically change the educational delivery system, as were instructional radio and television. Although each of these technology innovations had some impact on educational programs, they did little to change the fundamental nature of education itself. The Internet and computer technology, as the next generation of technological innovation to affect distance education, appears to have the power to significantly alter the education landscape.

In spite of the rapid growth in its use, there is considerable concern about the effectiveness of computer technology in education. Numerous studies comparing traditional classroom-based instruction with technology-supported instruction have found no significant differences in critical educational variables such as learning outcomes and student satisfaction (Clarke, 1999; Johnson, Aragon, Shaik, and Palma-Rivas, 2000; Navarro and Shoemaker, 1999; Smeaton and Keogh, 1999). A comprehensive book (Russell, 1999) and an up-to-date Web site (http://teleeducation.nb.ca/nosignificantdifference) contain a listing of over three hundred research reports, summaries, and papers on the effectiveness of technology-mediated distance learning. This comprehensive bibliography spans seven decades and highlights studies that reveal little or no significant impact of instructional technology on various educational variables.

The obvious conclusion from many studies in this field is that the technology used to support instruction has little impact on students' attainment of educational outcomes. The primary factor in any instructional initiative, regardless of format or venue, is the quality of the instructional design that is ultimately implemented. Based on the lack of evidence that technology significantly influences the learning process, scholars in the field of instructional technology now conclude that the technology used in an online program is not as important as other instructional factors, such as pedagogy and course design (Phipps and Merisotis, 1999). This is not a new idea, however, as Schramm stated in 1977: "Learning seems to be affected more by what is delivered than by the delivery medium" (p. 273).

This chapter describes a research and development effort that evolved during the creation of an HRD (human resource development) graduate program called HRE Online that was taught entirely online. The learning environment that was created to support HRE Online was based on the assumption that learning is a complex event that cannot be explained with a single theory of learning. Instead, we hypothesized that quality learning environments should be based on instructional principles that are derived from multiple learning theories. Through an analysis of existing literature and experienced-based practices throughout the development of HRE Online, we identified a set of instructional principles for online learning environments that are derived from a fusion of multiple theories of learning. Using these instructional principles as a framework, we then developed specific instructional strategies or techniques to be applied in an online learning environment.

Instructional Challenges for Online Course Designers

Innovations in instructional technology are often implemented in very traditional ways. For example, while television had the potential to significantly alter the way people were educated, its use as an instructional tool built on an existing instructional paradigm by providing a "talking head" that merely passed information to the student. Using this innovation in this way lacked creativity and ignored the power of the technology.

The same problem now seems to be occurring in online instruction. Instructional designers are creating online courses that are simple conversions of their equivalent face-to-face counterparts. Although educational innovations such as active learning, collaborative learning, project-based teaching, and situation learning have changed the nature of face-to-face instruction, online courses tend to build on very traditional views of learning. Often the primary goal of an online course is to transfer information from the instructor to the student by providing students with access to information and expecting them to demonstrate their learning on an exam. Examples of traditional forms of face-to-face instruction that have been converted for online delivery include recorded lectures, online readings, homework assignments, and online tests.

The growth of online instructional programs raises an interesting question for online course developers. Should online course designs follow the "traditional" models of instruction, or should innovative approaches be incorporated into online programs? If the answer is to design online courses that go beyond instruction as an information delivery system, the challenge for Web-based course developers becomes clear. Instructional designers need to look for innovative ways to support quality teaching and learning without succumbing to the temptation to have online instruction become direct instantiations of traditional forms of instruction. The challenge for instructional designers is to devise ways to incorporate the most effective and innovative instructional strategies in courses delivered over the Internet.

Instructional Principles for Online Learning Environments

In order to meet this challenge, instructional designers must examine their traditional perspectives and adopt a philosophy of teaching and learning that is appropriate for online instruction. This does not imply that traditional learning theories such as behaviorism should be tossed aside in favor of the more contemporary social-constructionist theories. Instructional designers need to match their desired learning goals and instructional methods to the appropriate learning theories. We argue that this new philosophy should build on a combination of learning theories rather than be confined to one preferred perspective (Johnson, 1997). For example, quality online learning environments should be made up of elements of behavioral learning theory (for example, using positive reinforcement and repetition), cognitive learning theory (for example, addressing multiple senses, presenting new information in motivating ways, limiting the amount of information presented, and connecting new information to prior knowledge), and social learning theory (for example, encouraging group interaction, peer assessment, and personal feedback). Adopting a synthesized theory of learning can have a synergistic result by integrating the most positive and powerful aspects of each individual learning theory into an online learning environment.

Specific aspects of adult learning theory guided the development of the pedagogical model that was used to develop the HRE Online master's degree program (Bandura, 1971; Cross, 1981; Knowles, 1984; Merriam and Caffarella, 1999; Vygotsky, 1978). Two conceptual models that were developed from an extensive study of the literature were reviewed. These two models were then synthesized into seven general principles that appear to be critical for quality learning environments (Johnson and Thomas, 1992; Johnson, 1997). We contend that powerful online learning environments need to contain a combination of these principles: (1) address individual differences, (2) motivate the student, (3) avoid information overload, (4) create a real-life context, (5) encourage social interaction, (6) provide hands-on activities, and (7) encourage student reflection (see Figure 3.1). This peda-

Figure 3.1. An Instructional Strategy Framework for Online Learning Environments

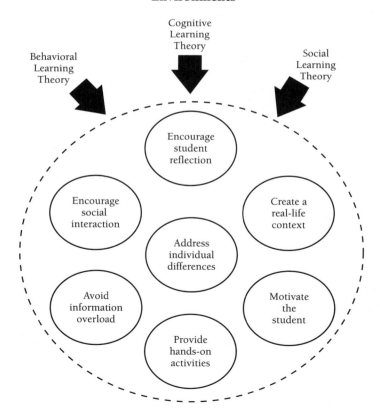

gogical model for online instruction was used to create the design template that is followed for each course in the HRE Online program.

The next section provides specific examples of instructional strategies that have been used in the HRE Online program. Each of these strategies highlights the importance and practical application of the seven principles of quality online learning environments.

Individual Differences. Differences among students within a learning context can be found in the areas of general skills, aptitude, information processing, and application of information to new situations. In addition, all learners differ in their ability to perform various education-based and real-world learning tasks. Consequently, the general abilities or preferences of the learner will affect his or her ability to achieve different learning outcomes. Individual differences specific to learning and instruction can be found in intelligence, cognitive controls, cognitive styles, learning styles, personality types, and prior knowledge (Jonassen and Grabowski, 1993). Recognition of individual differences has, for the most part, been taken into account and promoted through the instructional design template used in HRE Online. The following techniques and strategies have been used in our online courses to address individual differences.

Provide Content in Multiple Formats. This is done through the use of various communication technologies. Lectures are audiostreamed and synchronized with the applicable PowerPoint presentation. These lectures are also transcribed and posted in the course Web site, which is beneficial for students who travel and want to take the transcribed lecture with them to read. Content is also presented through WebBoard discussion groups, where students are required to share and discuss information with each other. Each course also has links to outside Web sites that provide supplemental material on the current topic.

Allow for Individual Locus of Control. All courses provide various means of navigation within the online course. Content can be accessed through links or a graphical organizer. Individuals can be as systematic or random in accessing course material as they desire. Although the course is built and presented in a hierarchical sequence, it does not have to be accessed in the same way, and students may even move through the course topics in random order.

Encourage Active and Collaborative Interaction. In light of the idea that the whole is greater than the sum of its parts, each course is designed with activities that are both individual- and group-based. Working within "virtual teams," students work together to solve problems, analyze cases, and develop group deliverables. These assignments allow individual ideas, perspectives, and experiences to be heard and collectively considered. The idea of "agreeing to disagree" is taught through these experiences.

Motivation. Motivation, in terms of student attention, relevance of content, confidence in one's ability to learn, and satisfaction with the learning experience are critical aspects of a learning environment (Keller and Suzuki,

1988). Instructors must be able to gain and maintain students' attention by providing an environment that is engaging and participative. Although keeping students' attention is critical, that attention cannot be maintained unless the students feel that the course material is relevant. In other words, the course content, activities, and assignments must be related to students' personal and professional goals. Students must also feel confident that they can be successful in the course and satisfied with their experience.

Strategies for enhancing student motivation in a Web-based environment can best be characterized as either novel and entertaining approaches or attempts to personalize the instruction. We have successfully used the following techniques to enhance the motivation of our online students.

Incorporate Games into the Online Environment. An example of a successful game for an online course is the popular television show "Who Wants to Be a Millionaire?" We have used this game during live synchronous sessions to summarize course content covered previously and to provide a sense of community among the students. The instructor plays the role of Regis Philbin, the game show host, and reads a question that requires the students to put a sequence of answers in the correct order. The students then type the correct order (for example, B, C, D, A) as quickly as they can into a WebBoard chat window. The student who first answers correctly becomes the contestant who calls a toll-free number so his or her voice can be patched through to the class. This provides live dialogue when the instructor asks a student the first of several multiple-choice questions. The student has the option of answering the question directly or, if unsure of the answer, can use one of two "lifelines." The lifeline "Ask the Audience" involves asking all students to post what they think is the correct answer in the chat space. The contestant can then use their colleagues' responses to select the correct answer. The contestant can also "Phone a Friend" by asking one particular student for help and then may respond by typing the answers in the chat space. The game continues until the student answers a predetermined number of questions correctly or responds with an incorrect answer. When this happens, another sequencing question is asked so another contestant can be selected.

Simulate a Radio Talk Show with Multiple DJs and "Call-In" Guests. In many online courses, the students spend much of the "class time" listening to the instructor through streaming audio or video technologies or in a live "Web cast" during a synchronous class session. As we all know, it can be both boring and difficult to listen to one voice for any length of time, especially when there are few visual cues to accompany the audio. To provide variety and a livelier online atmosphere, we have been successful having multiple speakers interact during these broadcasts to liven up the synchronous sessions.

Use Multimedia When Appropriate. Online courses tend to be primarily text-based forms of instruction. Although this may be preferable to some students, we must recognize that the students of today are different from those of the past. The MTV generation seems to prefer visual over verbal stimulation, and there is no excuse for not incorporating multimedia into technology-based learning systems. We have found that graphic images, photographs, and videos enhance student motivation. For example, in several of our courses we have created short QuickTime clips from popular movies and television shows that can be streamed over the Web. These clips provide entertaining examples that support the concepts and procedures being discussed in class and provide a nice break from the textual format that dominates current online environments.

Information Overload. Providing too much information in a short period of time contributes to memory overload, which makes learning difficult and leads to confusion and poor retention. Psychological studies show that most people can manage about seven "pieces" of information at one time without too much difficulty (Miller, 1956). Providing more than that amount of information at one time overloads short-term memory. Instructional designers need to follow the Rule of Seven, which suggests that the amount of information presented at one time should be limited to no more than seven pieces of content (Clement, 1985). The Rule of Seven suggests that instructional designers "chunk" instructional content into small groups and give students the opportunity to learn each "chunk" thoroughly before being presented with new information. Using this strategy will result in better understanding.

The following strategies have been used successfully in our online program.

Limit the Amount of Content and Number of Activities. By following the Rule of Seven, we help avoid memory overload by purposely limiting the amount of information and activities we provide in a course. For example, we ask instructors to break their lectures into ten- to twelve-minute "chunks" or segments. These short lectures are recorded and converted into streaming media for delivery to students. The shortness of the lectures makes it easier for students to absorb them in one sitting and forces the instructor to concentrate on only a few main concepts in each "mini" lecture. This approach also fits ideally with the concept of a learning cycle.

Organize Instruction Around Learning Cycles. The instructional design model for the HRE Online program uses learning cycles at the core of its modular approach. Each course has a hierarchical structure containing sections, modules, and learning cycles. This approach allows for easy updating of courses over time and the development of custom courses to meet different client-group needs. More important, this instructional design approach builds on theories of adult learning.

Each learning cycle is made up of three components. The first component provides the student with access to new content through a streamed audio or video file or by reading an online article. The last component of the learning cycle involves evaluating the learning outcomes through an activity involving self-assessment, peer assessment, or formal instructor assessment and feedback. Once the learning cycle is completed, a new cycle begins with the presentation of a new chunk of content, followed by new application and assessment activities.

Provide a Graphic Organizer for the Course. It is easy for students to get lost in any hypertext environment as they navigate through online courses that contain extensive layers of content distributed over multiple locations. To avoid the frustration and memory overload that can occur in a Web-based environment, we provide a visual representation of the course structure. This graphic organizer serves as a map for students as they navigate through various portions of the course. The graphic is also hyperlinked so students can move quickly to a desired location in the course by clicking directly on the image.

Contextual Learning. Context is an essential central element in learning because knowledge is a product of the activity, context, and culture in which it is developed and used (Brown, Collins, and Duguid, 1989). Wilson (1993) identifies three major premises of context and how these affect knowing and learning. The first is the idea that learning and thinking are social activities that are structured by constant interpersonal interaction. Second, the available tools within the particular situation significantly guide an individual's ability to think and learn. Third, human thinking is supported by interaction with the environment.

We offer the following recommendations to online instructors to promote contextual learning in the virtual classroom.

Create Virtual Learning Teams. At the start of each new course, students are placed in a virtual learning team consisting of three to four other classmates. This allows the instructor to replicate the group experience found in face-to-face settings. Students work together on weekly assignments and projects via conferencing systems, conference calls, e-mail, and instant messaging. This initiative provides a group context that is similar to what would be experienced in the face-to-face classroom.

Simulate Reality Using Appropriate Case Studies. Regardless of the delivery format, the more real-life examples that can be used, the better students will learn. Case studies are an excellent way to provide the context through which new learning can be developed. As with any situation when a case study is used, it is critical to choose cases that relate to the content of the course. In our online evaluation course, students are provided with a case describing a program in an organization that needs to be evaluated for effectiveness. Throughout the duration of the course, students are asked to design an evaluation around this case using the concepts, ideas, and procedures taken from the course materials. Students are provided with feedback through WebBoard discussions and weekly synchronous chat sessions.

Require Collaborative Projects with Schools, Businesses, or Other Organizations. Students are encouraged, when possible and appropriate, to develop course projects within the context of their work environment. This provides a real-life context in which to imbed application of the material. For example, in the online instructional design course, students develop a training package that represents six to eight hours of training time. The majority of the students choose to develop a training package that addresses a performance issue within their organization.

Social Learning. Social learning theory combines elements from both behaviorist and cognitive theories and posits that we learn best by interacting with others in social settings (Merriam and Caffarella, 1999). Behavioral learning theory contributes to social learning because people do not learn from observation alone but through imitation and reinforcement of what they observe. Cognitive theory focuses on the cognitive processes involved in the observation over the resulting behavior, with the idea that individuals can regulate their own behavior by recognizing consequences. Social learning is manifested through socialization, social roles, mentoring, and locus of learning. Instructors and peers serve as a model for new roles and behaviors within an educational context.

Online faculty have used the following strategies successfully to promote this perspective.

Create a Personal Connection with Students. The goal is for the instructor to be perceived as a real person in mediated communication. This perception is promoted several ways. Each course has an audiostreamed welcome message from the faculty member, which helps the student put a face with the voice. In addition, using humor and vocal variety, personalizing examples, addressing students by name, questioning, praising, initiating discussion, and encouraging feedback all help make this connection. Personal connection can also be made through the use of "relational icons" or "emoticons" made by combinations of punctuation marks.

Peer Review and Feedback. Feedback from fellow students is as important as instructor feedback. Therefore, students in many online classes are asked to provide a meta-evaluation of another student's work. The purpose of the activity is for students to help their peers by providing comments that help the person understand the areas that are clear and well done and the parts that need further development. This activity also models appropriate format for the particular assignment being developed.

Require and Facilitate Interaction. This may not seem like a new approach, but in the online environment it is easy for students to be passive, both in weekly assignments involving the group and during synchronous chat sessions. In addition to basing a percentage of the course grade on participation, other initiatives can be taken as well. One is to post an agenda of the upcoming week's synchronous session. This serves as an advanced organizer and allows students to come to class better prepared for interaction. Another technique is to post discussion questions prior to a synchronous session so students can think about the topic and be ready for a discussion. Throughout the week, students are required to review comments and ideas that have been posted by other students and respond to them in a virtual class discussion.

Two things are important to keep in mind. First, although the quantity of interactions is important (as measured by hits on the WebBoard), the quality of interaction is what should be stressed. If not, it becomes too easy for students to fall into the trap of providing comments that add little or no value to the discussion. Second, it is important that the instructor model the expected type of interaction by providing quality comments to the discussion as well.

Active Learning. There seems to be an assumed separation between knowing and doing in education (Brown, Collins, and Duguid, 1989), whereby knowing is valued over doing, and mental activity is valued over physical activity. However, cognitive theorists have challenged this perspective because the activities through which learning occurs are inseparable from cognition. In order for online instruction to be successful, some form of learner activity must be included.

Active learning can occur in many forms in an online environment. Discovery learning, project-based learning, and cooperative learning are common techniques for engaging students in activities that involve considerable amounts of creativity, decision making, and problem solving. Each of these instructional approaches emphasizes the importance of learning from goal-driven and activity-based experience. Because these types of activities usually take time to complete, they provide for sustained thinking about specific problems over long periods of time.

The following are specific examples of how active learning can be applied in an online environment.

Organize Online Courses Around Projects. Because HRD is a constantly evolving, applied field of study, it is reasonable to design an online HRD course with a heavy emphasis on the application of the skills and procedures needed by the HRD professional. The best way to accomplish this in an online environment is through a project-based approach. Application-rich courses can be designed around major projects and specific activities to be completed in order to create a final product. For example, in the instructional design course where students are expected to create a complete training module, they complete many tasks, such as conducting a needs assessment, developing training plans, and creating instructional media. By adopting a project-based approach, the online instructor can easily incorporate the concept of active learning into a virtual environment instead of providing the typical "read and write" online course.

Think-Pair-Share in a Virtual Environment. Having online students work in groups of two or three within a virtual environment is a great way to keep students active and focused on their learning. Think-pair-share is an active learning technique used in many face-to-face classes but is rarely used in a virtual environment. The goal is to help students organize prior knowledge, brainstorm questions, or summarize, integrate, and apply new information. This strategy can be used in both synchronous and asynchronous situations.

Use Small-Group Discussions During Synchronous Sessions. Although few online programs seem to rely on synchronous class sessions, they can provide powerful opportunities for student interaction. We conduct weekly synchronous sessions in our program in which the instructor performs a live audio broadcast to the students over the Web while the students interact with the instructor and other students in a group chat space. Although this in itself encourages active learning, incorporating small-group interactions into the large-group discussions further enhances it. This is accomplished by having the instructor describe a discussion activity to the class and then asking them to enter their private "virtual team" chat space to discuss and complete the assignment. A specific time is given when the students are expected to return to the class chat space and share the major points of their discussion with the rest of the class. Although this technique is commonly used in many face-to-face classes, it is a unique, yet underused strategy in an online learning environment.

Reflective Learning. Mezirow defines *learning* as "the process of making a new or revised interpretation of the meaning of an experience, which guides subsequent understanding, appreciation, and action" (1990, p. 1). This process of reexamining and revising one's understanding occurs through reflection, which allows one's ideas, understandings, and experiences to be reviewed and challenged (Preskill and Torres, 1999) and leads to a change in one's values, strategies, and assumptions. Through reflection, individuals can correct their misconceptions by revisiting their beliefs and challenging the nature of their knowledge. Watkins and Marsick (1993) see reflection as a key to continuous learning.

The following three strategies can be used to promote reflective learning.

Provide Extensive and Timely Feedback. Although most instructors already know this, it is important to remember that the online environment removes some of the human "checks and balances" that face-to-face students have with the instructor. Although the opportunity to ask questions and have interaction with the instructor is relatively equal, feedback received through physical distance, eye contact, facial expressions, and personal topics of conversation is not present for these individuals. Therefore, it becomes even more important that the instructor take time to provide feedback that is detailed enough to paint a complete evaluative picture. This includes addressing not only the areas that were weak or in need of improvement but providing praise for the areas that were done well. Instructors are encouraged to get this feedback to the students no later than a week after the assignment is turned in.

Incorporate "One Minute Papers" and "Muddiest Point" into Class. "One Minute Papers" are short writing exercises in which students are asked to reflect on a particular topic as a form of knowledge assessment activity. Students are asked to post a quick list of the new knowledge they gained through a particular session. The "Muddiest Point" activity allows students to identify the areas of confusion or uncertainty or to raise additional questions around the content of the session. Both of these activities benefit the students and instructor by providing feedback on what was clear and what may need further attention through the use of reflection.

Online Diaries or Reflective Journals. Diaries and journals promote continuous reflection throughout the course. Entries can be self-directed or promoted by an issue, question, or experience posed by the instructor. Journals allow students to reflectively interact with various course topics and experiences and, as noted earlier, critically examine how their values, beliefs, and attitudes fit with the material. This is a way that promotes growth beyond what regular instructor-and-student interactions provide.

Conclusion

The instructional strategy framework discussed in this chapter is clearly a work in progress. Although the framework is based on well-recognized theories of learning and represents a synthesis of ideas from multiple perspectives, it is not fully developed, nor is it all-inclusive. Additional principles will be added as the online program continues to develop and evolve. The specific techniques for applying the instructional principles highlighted in this chapter are currently in use in the HRE Online courses and continue to be enhanced each time they are implemented. The possibilities for application of the instructional strategy framework are only limited by the creativity and energy of the instructional designers and course instructors.

The purpose of this chapter was to present a perspective of online teaching and learning strategies that looks beyond the traditional paradigm of instruction. Once such a perspective is adopted, instructional designers can incorporate the key elements that are needed in quality online learning environments.

References

Bandura, A. *Social Learning Theory.* New York: General Learning Press, 1971.

Brown, J. S., Collins, A., and Duguid, P. "Situated Cognition and the Culture of Learning." *Educational Researcher,* 1989, *18*(1), 32–42.

Clarke, D. "Getting Results with Distance Education." *The American Journal of Distance Education,* 1999, *12*(1), 38–51.

Clement, F. J. "The Rule of Seven Revisited." *Performance and Instruction Journal,* 1985, *24*(2), 6–8.

Cross, K. P. *Adults As Learners.* San Francisco: Jossey-Bass, 1981.

Garrison, D. R. "The Role of Technology in Distance Education." In *New Directions for Continuing Education,* no. 36. San Francisco: Jossey-Bass, 1987.

Johnson, S. D. "Learning Technological Concepts and Developing Intellectual Skills." *International Journal of Technology and Design Education,* 1997, *7,* 161–180.

Johnson, S. D., Aragon, S. R., Shaik, N., and Palma-Rivas, N. "Comparative Analysis of Learner Satisfaction and Learning Outcomes in Online and Face-to-Face Learning

Environments." *Journal of Interactive Learning Research,* 2000, *11,* 29–49.

Johnson, S. D., and Thomas, R. G. "Technology Education and the Cognitive Revolution." *The Technology Teacher,* 1992, *51*(4), 7–12.

Jonassen, D. H., and Grabowski, B. L. *Handbook of Individual Differences, Learning, and Instruction.* Hillsdale, N.J.: Erlbaum, 1993.

Keller, J. M., and Suzuki, K. "Use of the ARCS Motivation Model in Courseware Design." In D. Jonassen (ed.), *Instructional Designs for Microcomputer Courseware.* Hillsdale, N.J.: Erlbaum, 1988.

Knowles, M. *The Adult Learner: A Neglected Species.* (3rd ed.) Houston, Tex.: Gulf Publishing, 1984.

Lewis, L., Snow, K., Farris, E., Levin, D., and Greene, B. *Distance Education at Postsecondary Education Institutions: 1997–98* (NCES Report no. 2000–013). Washington, D.C.: U.S. Department of Education, National Center for Education Statistics, 1999.

Merriam, S. B., and Caffarella, R. S. *Learning in Adulthood: A Comprehensive Guide.* (2nd ed.) San Francisco: Jossey-Bass, 1999.

Mezirow, J. "How Critical Reflection Triggers Transformative Learning." In J. Mezirow (ed.), *Fostering Critical Reflection in Adulthood.* San Francisco: Jossey-Bass, 1990.

Miller, G. A. "The Magical Number Seven, Plus or Minus Two." *Psychological Review,* 1956, *63,* 81–97.

Navarro, P., and Shoemaker, J. "The Power of Cyberlearning: An Empirical Test." *Journal of Computing in Higher Education,* 1999, *11*(1), 29–54.

Phipps, R., and Merisotis, J. *What's the Difference? A Review of Contemporary Research on the Effectiveness of Distance Learning in Higher Education* (report from The Institute for Higher Education Policy), Apr. 1999. Retrieved from http://www.ihep.com/PUB.htm.

Preskill, H., and Torres, R. T. *Evaluative Inquiry for Learning in Organizations.* Thousand Oaks, Calif.: Sage, 1999.

Russell, T. L. *The No Significant Difference Phenomenon.* Raleigh: North Carolina State University, 1999.

Smeaton, A., and Keogh, G. "An Analysis of the Use of Virtual Delivery of Undergraduate Lectures." *Computers and Education,* 1999, *32,* 83–94.

Vygotsky, L. S. *Mind in Society.* Cambridge, Mass.: Harvard University Press, 1978.

Waits, T., Lewis, L., and Greene, B. *Distance Education at Degree-Granting Postsecondary Institutions: 2000–2001* (NCES Report no. 2003–017). Washington, D.C.: U.S. Department of Education, National Center for Education Statistics, 2003.

Watkins, K. E., and Marsick, V. J. *Sculpting a Learning Organization.* San Francisco: Jossey-Bass, 1993.

Wilson, A. L. "The Promise of Situated Cognition." In *New Directions for Adult and Continuing Education,* no. 57. San Francisco: Jossey-Bass, 1993.

Scott D. Johnson is a professor and head of human resource education at the University of Illinois at Urbana-Champaign, specializing in instructional design, instructional methods, and online learning.

Steven R. Aragon is an assistant professor in the Department of Human Resource Education at the University of Illinois at Urbana-Champaign, specializing in postsecondary education (community college), teaching and learning models for postsecondary minority and nontraditional students, and minority student development in community college settings.

4

The challenges and opportunities that online education and training present for instructors is discussed, along with strategies that can help instructors succeed in online environments.

Preparing Instructors for Online Instruction

Adam D. Fein, Mia C. Logan

> Man's mind once stretched by a new idea, never regains its original dimensions.
>
> Oliver Wendell Holmes

Imagine that you have used an existing process for a long time, and now you are being asked to use a new process to get the same results. You might be an instructor who has been teaching for fifteen years and using a set way of designing your curriculum and courses. But now you have been asked to redesign some of your courses to be incorporated into an online environment. You have never designed an online course and do not know where to start. This is a very large—possibly overwhelming—challenge for you.

Instructors face this challenge today more than ever before. It is a new challenge that requires a different way of thinking. Currently, face-to-face classroom-oriented instructors are expected to stretch themselves when it comes to online instruction—a very different medium—to facilitate learning.

Teaching in an online environment can present new challenges and opportunities for instructors (Paloff and Pratt, 1999). This chapter explores what some of these potential challenges are and discusses some strategies that can help instructors flourish under these new parameters.

Transitioning from face-to-face instruction to online learning can be a difficult change to make and requires making a paradigm shift (Bates, 1997). Instructors need to remain open-minded and realize that there will be some frustrations (Paloff and Pratt, 2001). Embracing these changes and understanding the strengths, weaknesses, and differences in online instruction will lead to successful learning for your students in a relevant anytime-any-where format.

Initial Framework

Before any design can be attempted, an initial framework must be in place, and the instructor must have the support of his or her organization or institution. Due to a heavier management workload, design, delivery, and follow-up should not be left to the course instructor alone. If you, as the instructor, are left to support your project alone, you run a high risk of creating inconsistencies and, eventually, failures in learning. Do not attempt online instruction without proper support. Another problem is that instructors can be faced with internal resistance to change, which often occurs when we fear a new way of doing something or a lack of knowledge or skills to make that change.

Many face-to-face classroom instructors do not want to be online instructors. In the experience of one of the coauthors of this chapter as an online coordinator of two master's-level programs, the courses that were rated the highest by the students were the courses where the instructor made the necessary changes to adapt the classroom course into the online environment. Not only did they make changes in the initial design stage but each semester they taught the course, they made adjustments based on student feedback and personal experience. If the instructor is truly interested in teaching online, modifications of the classroom version of the course must be made.

The instructor must shift from the role of content provider to content facilitator, gain comfort and proficiency in using the Web as the primary teacher-student link, and learn to teach effectively without the visual control provided by direct eye contact (Smith, Ferguson, and Caris, 2002). It is clear that teaching in the online environment is an entirely different animal (Darling, 2000). Hence, it is important to make sure instructors are selected because they want to work in an online arena and have the skills, knowledge, and support they need to do so.

Design

One of the first questions the instructor should ask is, Is this course to be newly designed, or will I be teaching a course that has previously been designed by another instructor? (Paloff and Pratt, 2001). Teaching another instructor's course can lead to a different set of instructions, such as how much content creation there will be. Other questions: What were the concerns and issues of past semesters? Do I have permission from the former instructor to modify the structure? For a previously designed course, those questions must be answered, but for the purpose of this chapter we will assume that you are starting your instruction from scratch.

Challenges. Online education presents many challenges. In designing your instruction, you must be aware that the initial preparation can be extremely time-consuming. Web-based distance classes require considerably more work, often including hundreds of hours of up-front work, to set the course up (Smith, Ferguson, and Caris, 2001). Entering raw content into the learning management system can take quite a lot of time. In many situations, the content has to be adjusted for online viewing, including adding hotlinks. Exams must be converted into an online assessment system, and the instructor must decide where and how the data will be submitted. Will they be linked directly to a grading system? How will the instructor access the material? If the site is password-protected, how will students access it? Will they use their work or student ID, or does the assessment system require them to memorize another ID and password? Will students be logging on with dial-up modems or behind firewalls?

Lectures traditionally given face-to-face will have to be prerecorded for asynchronous delivery. An instructor who is not used to lecturing into a monitor may take a second or third pass before becoming comfortable. These are just a few of the time-consuming challenges that face the new online instructor in the design phase.

The technology itself is a challenge during the design of online learning. Instructors must understand that the technologies they use can and will cause problems. They will have to learn the technology themselves, as well as seek out support from IT staff. Instructors should not hesitate to rely on these specialists to help them with the design and delivery processes; however, it is also vital that the instructor understand the various technologies that will make up the institution's online learning environment. This can often be difficult; in the traditional classroom, most instructors do not have to rely on others to ensure that their classes are successfully designed and delivered. Depending on the instructor's experience with technology, this can be a steep learning curve.

Many instructors have more than enough technology experience, but there are also pitfalls for being too tech-savvy. When one of the coauthors first became coordinator, he wanted to modernize the entire program in one week: more graphics, more audio and video—in other words, more bells and whistles. What he quickly learned was that the design of online instruction can benefit from cutting-edge technology, but it must be used sparingly and tested vigorously before deployment. Bells and whistles are nice, but successful student interactions through reliable servers with near 100 percent uptime, easy-to-use applications, and fluid course navigation are much more important. Simplicity, transparency, and reliability were preferred, despite minor glitches and downtime. Do not overuse technology, be wary of first or beta versions of catchy products, and you will be able to keep the focus of the instruction on the learner.

When designing the course, the instructor needs to come from a place of learner-centeredness. The focus has to be on the learner and not the technology. The learners need to be challenged with a problem to solve, a project to complete, or a dilemma that needs to be resolved. The instructor needs to facilitate an environment in which learners can discover the content on their own, carrying out assignments and creating learning opportunities that are self-directed (Hootstein, 2002). Although technologies hold strong potential for remote collaboration, the power of expanded learning hours by accessing course contents anytime is the most widely used dimension of online learning at present.

Online instructors have to create problems that are realistic to the learner. The information or content needs to be adapted to the purposes and tasks to which it will be applied. A more project-based approach should be favored over a traditional didactic approach so that learners can ask questions and stay engaged in the process. An instructor can use case studies, collaborative activities, small-group dialogue, and simulations to engage them in problem solving. Instructors ask questions and assist the learners through the process.

A third challenge in the design of online instruction lies in keeping focused on students. As stated previously, a critical component of an online class is regular and frequent participation by the students and the instructor. Your main role, as instructor, is to ensure and facilitate a high degree of participation and interactivity by the students (Fredrickson, Clark, and Hoehner, 2002). This can be done through the use of e-mail, newsgroups, listservs, chat rooms, instant messaging, conferencing, and multiuser discussions.

Online instructors should help learners foster collaborative skills through project management, time management, consensus building, and leadership (Hootstein, 2002). If instructors truly want to keep a high degree of student focus, they must not directly transfer their traditional lecture-format material into an online format without making adjustments to activities and assignments. Developing an online course does not mean that you take traditional course syllabi, lecture notes, or PowerPoint presentations and simply place them intact on a Web page (Fredrickson, Clark, and Hoehner, 2002). In order to design successful online instruction, one has to develop appropriate resources in which the pedagogy matches the learning design.

As we have discussed, the design of an online course is very different from a face-to-face classroom course. Instructional design is important in e-learning "because you have a machine in front of you that has the power to put people to sleep, so the courses have to be compelling," says Carliner (2002). The design needs to include more interactivity within the online environment.

Strategies. Let's look at some potential design strategies that will help instructors confront the challenges in the online environment. Hands-on learning will help instructors learn the technology they will be required to use for the class. Instructors are strongly recommended to take an online course or attend a videoconference to see what it's like to be a learner (Mantyla, 2002). This should be done prior to the development of the online course.

According to Hoostein (2002), the goal of the instructor is "to make the technology transparent." This allows the learner to focus on learning and not get stifled with technology issues. The more instructors are familiar with the technology, the higher their degree of comfort, and the more they will be able to solely focus on the learners.

Flexibility is a helpful strategy to keep in mind when learning the new technologies and the pitfalls that may occur along the way. Instructors need to remain amenable to what can happen with the technology. For example, one participant may not be able to access a page that the class is currently viewing. This is a common occurrence, especially during synchronous hours. Using a technology support staff and being familiar with the online learning environment is essential in these situations. When handled correctly, this will not only foster a trusting relationship with the learner but will allow for fewer content-based interaction interruptions by not hindering class flow. Many unforeseen circumstances can occur with technology, and instructors need to plan for them in advance, during the design phase, so that they are prepared when the content is delivered.

Securing a back-up plan in case the technology fails is yet another important strategy in the design phase. Who is responsible for your servers? Whom do you contact if they go down right before class? How do you contact them? Will they be monitoring the servers 24/7? During the synchronous sessions? Your learners must also know where to go when technology is not functioning properly. Having at least three avenues for the client to contact the instructor and support staff is vital. Instant messenger office hours, a tech-help e-mail address, a 1–800 number, and emergency chat boards are all reliable means for back-up and emergency strategies. The instructor should have all of these in place before delivering the course.

Perhaps the most important strategy in the design of online instruction is to include an assistant or cofacilitator to provide support for the aforementioned time-consuming tasks. Having enough advance time to design your instruction before going "live" (start *at least* a few months before your course will be offered) is essential. A plan must be in place to organize your support staff so that they understand their roles and know how they can support the instructor.

A key cog to this plan would be to create a leader guide or online assistant handbook that specifically outlines production tasks, expectations, and online terminology and may even include application tutorials. For example, include instructions for writing on the white board, conducting the warm-up exercises, and posting text into the chat area. The guide should be very specific and cover the when, the why, and the what. Formatting the guide so that tasks can be quickly identified will also help the instructor be better prepared for the problems that arise when an assistant may not be available. In designing this handbook and examining proposed tasks, the instructor can make informed decisions about which items are manageable without help and which need to be modified or shared.

It is important to meet with the support staff at least a month ahead of the first week of class to walk through and discuss the exercises and course structure. This meeting is best held in a face-to-face format so that the assistant can prepare for exactly how the course will function on a weekly basis and become clearer about the overall course delivery and management plan of the instructor. This will not only allow the assistant to become familiar with the content but will also foster trust. One of the most important factors in a successful online course is creating an environment of trust between the instructor and the support staff. The instructor-assistant relationship should represent a true team. For example, if the assistant suggests that the trainer take a moment to review the questions in the chat area, the trainer needs to trust that the issues raised are worth considering.

Other issues that the instructor and support staff should discuss include how to respond to content questions, emergency procedures, chat room procedures, process checks, course ground rules, and so on. For example, the assistant needs to know how to respond to a participant who may arrive to class late or leave early. If someone logs on twenty minutes into a synchronous hour, should the assistant log that information for the instructor? The assistant must be prepared with a variety of options in order to keep the course moving according to schedule. Discussing these issues in advance will help provide guidance to the support staff and will be invaluable during delivery.

A final strategy in the design process is to prepare for capturing student focus in a distance environment. Many of the most successful online courses that our coauthor has assisted with provide multiple media types for the same instructional contents, such as PowerPoint slides, transcripts, and pre-recorded audio to address different learning styles and hold the students' interest. Instructional design is knowing your audience, knowing your content, knowing what about that content your audience needs to know, and presenting it in a way that's logical and compelling (Carliner, 2002). In order to make the course interesting, the instructor might want to include online guests in their classes, authors of articles, or experts in the field, who may reside at a distance yet participate in online, threaded discussion (Smith, Ferguson, and Caris, 2001).

When designing the course, it is best to focus on a problem-based approach. Instructors will need to aid the learners with resources and expertise that will help them solve problems. Conferencing accessibility will assist with this approach. Using e-mail, teleconferencing, Web databases, and audio- and videoconferencing will help increase interaction among the participants. Through these tools, learners will be able to solve problems in a creative way.

You are now ready to deliver your course.

Delivery

As we have discussed, instructors must manage online courses differently from the way they do it in a classroom. When delivering the course, their role has to change to accommodate the needs of online participants. Instructors may have to pay attention to cues that are different in an online atmosphere. The instructor is a vital part of the success of the distance learning event and needs to think of delivering training as a collaborative way of supporting the needs of the learners (Mantyla, 2000).

Challenges. Initial delivery challenges in the online environment include but are not limited to (1) having better listening and tracking skills, (2) asking more questions, and (3) spending extra time and effort engaging and enhancing the dialogue among the learners.

Other challenges lie within the synchronous online learning environment:

- The tool-set changes from flipcharts and LCD (liquid crystal display) projectors to interactive white boards, chat rooms, and application sharing.
- Short program times of one to two hours minimize an instructor's ability to make adjustments when the class strays from the schedule.
- The languages of eye contact and body movement are eliminated, and new cues fight for the instructor's attention, including chat between participants and private off-line questions sent to the instructor, as well as participants' white board activity, application sharing, and Web browsing.
- Participants rely on trainers for help with technical problems, from determining why content isn't synchronized to resolving computer crashes (Hoffman, 2001).

Instructor-to-student feedback may be the greatest challenge of online instruction delivery. As an instructor, one should focus on providing an environment that encourages feedback. This is a vital part of online delivery because often learners can feel isolated and detached due to the lack of face-to-face time and the absence of nonverbal signals.

A final challenge in the delivery of online instruction is staying organized throughout the course. Keeping the master course schedule updated, managing due dates, holding online office hours, and communicating with your support staff are key challenges that must be met to ensure a successful experience for your students.

Strategies. There are a number of strategies one can use to meet delivery challenges. Communicating with your support staff during the instruction is a key delivery strategy. Debriefing the weekly experiences is vital to the instructor-assistant relationship. After a live event, share notes about what was successful and what could be improved. This formative assessment of the course will sustain continued improvements. Make sure you document lessons learned for different instructors and assistants who may support the class in the future (Hofmann, 2001).

During delivery, while the instructor is teaching the course, the support staff's main function will be to troubleshoot; this will keep the flow and agenda fluid. An assistant could support learners getting logged in to class, administrative concerns, and technical difficulties (Duckworth, 2001).

This assistant can help transform synchronous time into trouble-free, fast-moving, interactive events that keep learners involved and the instructor on track. Other key tasks for an assistant might include handling technical questions and problems and managing messages in the chat room.

Quite a bit of crucial interaction can occur in the chat and message areas that must be captured and archived. For example, often after an instructor posts a question, five to ten different participants start sending questions at the same time, and the instructor cannot answer all of them. The support staff can help the instructor choose the most relevant inquiries and move forward. The assistant can watch for signals from participants, answer questions, and alert the instructor if his or her involvement is needed. The assistant's role can include scribing on the white board and warming up the participants before class begins. In short, the instructor can stay focused on content while the assistant takes care of everything else (Hoffman, 2001).

Another delivery strategy is to use new applications that may be different from the traditional classroom tools. Discussion boards, such as Web-Board, provide a forum for both synchronous and asynchronous discussions and are an essential tool for exchanging ideas. A discussion board helps students get their questions answered. Divide your discussion board into a weekly forum, such as Week 1, Week 2, and so on. Providing structure to the board can eliminate confusion and help learners organize their work.

According to Fredrickson, Clark, and Hoehner (2002), the critical components of the discussion board include instructor-directed threads, participant participation, graded participant participation, participant behavior, and instructor participation.

Through instructor-directed threads, an instructor can lead the conversation and ensure that all topics are covered. Student participation is a critical component because it requires regular and frequent participation by both the students and the instructor. The instructor can facilitate and ensure that a high degree of participation and activity will occur. Graded student participation requires regularly posting productive comments that advance the knowledge of the learning community. Participant behavior involves having the group develop some boundaries around dialogues on the discussion board. Instructor participation is vital to the success of the online course, but instructors' comments should not exceed 15 percent of the total postings for the course.

In addition to discussion boards, other components that are vital to the delivery strategy are an online syllabus or master schedule, listservs, rosters, a technical assistance center, curriculum map, an announcements area, and a clear course structure. The syllabus or master schedule serves as a contract for students, as well as a guide that provides them with links to access other course features. Every instructor should have a listserv that the instructor and the students can use to send e-mails to each other and to the class. A roster or teams-people page allows students in the class to obtain photos, e-mail addresses, current work backgrounds, and educational history. Personal information is optional but recommended, particularly for the programs that are 100 percent online, to help foster a virtual team environment. Technical support information can be posted on a Web site to assist students in obtaining help in the event of technical difficulties. This page should be updated frequently and include a "Top/Recent Issues" link.

Announcements need to be posted somewhere for students to see—on a home page, an intro page, or a discussion board conference. Announcements should also be updated regularly. Even when the instructor does not have an announcement, participants can preview upcoming classes, suggested readings, and reminders. If instructors use the announcement section regularly, participation in the course increases (Fredrickson, Clark, and Hoehner, 2002).

E-learning delivery must include a clear course structure. Chunking information into manageable modules will provide for the greatest amount of learning. Weekly lessons provided to the student should include asynchronous audio lectures, graphic slides, and a transcript. The lecture notes can provide links to reference materials, activities, notes, outlines, lesson assessments, additional readings, and an evaluation survey (Meyen, Tangen, and Lian, 1999).

The final delivery strategy is attending to the challenge of timely and specific feedback. Feedback provides guidance to learners on ways to improve their performance. Feedback can be delivered via e-mail, on a discussion board, or within a student tracking and grading system. From the very beginning of the course, the instructor should foster a high-quality feedback environment by establishing an expectation around the importance of instructor-student and student-student feedback. Open communication is important for the learners because they need to be supported in receiving answers to their questions via e-mail in a timely manner. The instructor needs to plan on checking and responding to e-mail on a regular schedule that is posted for the participant (Orde, Andrews, and Awad, 2001). E-mail, if not managed properly, can become overwhelming in a short period of time, particularly for an online course. One strategy that can help manage feedback is to set up a Frequently Asked Questions (FAQ) page. A FAQ page can facilitate self-direction for the learner in answering their questions.

Follow-Up

There are many advantages to online instruction once a course is completed. The content can be stored, retrieved, and disseminated anytime-anywhere, as opposed to the face-to-face course in which such interactions are time- and place-dependent and perishable.

Challenges. "If you develop your courses properly, including give-and-take with users, you will have made some basic decisions about critical issues such as screen design that you can leverage in future projects" (Carliner, 2002). Although this is true, prior to the design, development, and delivery of your online instruction, you do not want to adhere to what one faculty member has loosely termed the "in-the-can" syndrome.

In-the-can syndrome can be defined as allowing your course to remain unchanged as you continue to teach it over time. This is a major challenge to online instructors. It is very easy for an instructor to fail to revisit their online content. Lectures have been recorded, assignments have been set, exams have been programmed, and content has been archived; it is easy for the instructor to simply change the dates and teach it again. The gain for the instructor comes when the course is actually delivered.

Strategies. Once again, the most successful online learning experiences that some of the coauthor's students have shared with him are of the instructors who choose to avoid the in-the-can syndrome by consistently renewing their course. Using summative feedback and personal evaluation, the instructor should make adjustments to the learning content each time it is taught. Maybe the students found that the introduction lecture was weak, the guest speaker in Week 5 did not hold their attention, the midterm exam when translated to online format was too short; many improvements can be made through basic evaluation principles. Instructor evaluations can be administered online. Continuous student-to-instructor feedback will create a stronger learning environment and support the needs of the student for future instruction.

Conclusion

Instructors are faced with many new challenges when teaching in the online learning environment. There are key strategies one must follow during the design, delivery, and follow-up of instruction. We have discussed potential pitfalls and some ways to strategize within the new medium. As technology changes, we will be faced with new hurdles in the online teaching arena. Embracing these changes and understanding the strengths, weaknesses, and differences in online instruction will lead to successful learning for your students in a relevant anytime-anywhere format.

References

Bates, A. W. "The Impact of Technological Change on Open and Distance Learning." *Distance Education,* 1997, *18*(1) 93–109.

Carliner, S. *Instructional Design Is Even More Important in E-Learning.* American Society for Training and Development, Nov. 2002. Retrieved from http://www.knowledge-media.com/synergy/knowmgmt/moreinfo, Jan. 16, 2003.

Darling, L. "The Life and Times of an E-Trainer." *Learning Circuits by American Society for Training and Development,* 2000. Retrieved from http www.learningcircuits.org/may2000/lesley.html, Nov. 5, 2002.

Duckworth, C. L. "An Instructor's Guide to Live E-Learning." *Learning Circuits by American Society of Training and Development,* 2001. Retrieved from www.learningcircuits.org/2001/jul2001/duckworth.html, Nov. 5, 2002.

Fredrickson, S., Clark, B., and Hoehner, P. "Now That the Students Are Here, What Am I Going To Do? A Primer for the Online Instructor: Part 2." *Learning and Leading with Technology,* 2002, 29(7), 18–21.

Hoffman, J. "Synchronous Team Teaching: Put Your Heads Together." *Learning Circuits by American Society of Training and Development,* 2001. Retrieved from www.learningcircuits.org/2001/nov2001/elearn.html, Nov. 5, 2002.

Hoostein, E. "Wearing Four Pairs of Shoes: The Roles of E-Learning Facilitators." *Learning Circuits by American Society for Training and Development,* 2002. Retrieved from www.learningcircuits.org/2002/oct2002/elearn.html, Nov. 5, 2002.

Mantyla, K. "Who Wants to Be a Distance Trainer?" *Learning Circuits by American Society of Training and Development,* 2000. Retrieved from www.learningcircuits.org/jul2000/jul2000_elearn.html, Nov. 5, 2002.

Mantyla, K. "How to Select and Train Distance Learning Instructors." *Quiet Power,* 2002. Retrieved from http://www.quietpower.com/article3.asp, July 29, 2003.

Meyen, E. L., Tangen, P., and Lian, C. H. "Developing Online Instruction: Partnership Between Instructors and Technical Developers." *Journal of Special Education Technology,* 1999, 14(1), 18–31.

Orde, B. J., Andrews, J., and Awad, A. "Online Course Development: Summative Reflections." *International Journal of Instructional Media,* 2001, 28(4), 397–403.

Paloff, R., and Pratt, K. *Building Learning Communities in Cyberspace.* San Francisco: Jossey-Bass, 1999.

Paloff, R., and Pratt, K. *Lessons Learned from the Cyberspace Classroom.* San Francisco: Jossey-Bass, 2001.

Smith, G. G., Ferguson, D., and Caris, M. "Teaching College Courses On Line vs. Face-to-Face." *T.H.E. Journal,* 2001, 28(9), 18–26.

ADAM D. FEIN *is the human resource education (HRE) online coordinator at the University of Illinois, Urbana-Champaign.*

MIA C. LOGAN *is a partner and consultant with LTD Unlimited, located in Albuquerque, New Mexico.*

5

Recent literature has shown that social presence is one of the most significant factors in improving instructional effectiveness and building a sense of community. This chapter examines strategies for creating social presence within online environments.

Creating Social Presence in Online Environments

Steven R. Aragon

During the last decade, the Internet has significantly changed the way learning is delivered and facilitated in both educational and noneducational settings. Advocates of Internet-based instruction are largely positive and optimistic about its potential. But before it can be fully accepted by the mainstream public and educational community, many challenges must be addressed. Primary among these challenges is how to meet "the expectations and needs of both the instructor and the student and how to design online courses so they provide a satisfying and effective learning environment" (Johnson, Aragon, Shaik, and Palma-Rivas, 2000, p. 31).

According to Bibeau (2001), teaching and learning functions are inherently social endeavors; therefore, it is beneficial to understand the various effects of the geographic, temporal, and psychological distance between instructors and participants. The lens through which these distances are examined is that of social presence theory. This chapter examines definitions of social presence, the benefits of social presence on learning, and strategies for increasing social presence within online environments.

Prior to proceeding into the discussion of social presence, it is important to acknowledge the fact that recent thinking views social presence as one variable among many that contributes to building a sense of community among learners at a distance. Rovai (2001) presents a model of community that, in addition to social presence, suggests that student-instructor ratio, transactional distance, instructor immediacy, lurking, social equality, collaborative learning, group facilitation, and self-directed learning all have an impact on the sense of community within online environments. In a subsequent paper, Rovai (2002) modifies this framework by proposing transactional distance, social presence, social quality, small-group activities, group facilitation, teaching style and learning stage, and community size as positive correlates to a sense of community.

It is important to acknowledge the recent thinking connected to social presence in order to illustrate the context in which it fits and to avoid leaving the impression with the reader that social presence is the only ingredient by which successful online environments thrive. However, social presence has been made the sole focus of this chapter because I believe it is one of the first components that must be established in order to initiate learning in an online environment.

The Internet and Social Isolation

Before presenting the literature-based definition of social presence, take a few moments and place yourself in the following scenario—one many of us have experienced at one time or another. The context and actors may have been different, but the experience and feelings are the same. This scenario helps to illustrate what social presence is and the role it plays in helping us become engaged in situations involving the interaction with others.

Think about the last time you attended a professional development conference that you had never attended before, or the first day on a new job, in a new class, or in a training session sponsored by your place of work or an outside training organization; or perhaps you traveled to a new country. Think about all the new faces that surrounded you. Think about not knowing the ground rules or the accepted protocol of the particular context. Think about not knowing the "language" of the group, whether this was literally or figuratively true. Although you might have felt excited, you were probably anxious and uneasy as well, based on the situation being new. You might have also experienced feelings of loneliness or depression.

Now think about the various ways you went about easing your level of anxiety. Did you initiate a conversation with someone, or did someone initiate a conversation with you? Did you take some time just to "hang out" and observe? Did you look for people who were dressed in a similar way as you or appeared to be similar to you in terms of job position, education level, or socioeconomic status? What types of questions did you ask and of whom? Did you try to find people you already knew, or was there possibly some type of buddy system present in which you were assigned to someone who would show you the ropes? Regardless of your approach, I'm guessing that within a fairly short period of time, you became comfortable in this new social environment, and your comfort level continued to increase over time as a result of continued positive social interaction.

Finally, think about how you would have felt had you not connected socially with others in your new situation and context. Would it have been enjoyable? Would it have been one of the most miserable or boring experiences of your life? Would you have found some way to remove yourself from this situation and get back to your "real world?"

When we connect with others in new social situations, we create social presence or a degree of interpersonal contact (Gunawardena and Zittle, 1997). The challenge in online learning environments is facilitating this degree of interpersonal contact with the instructor and other participants. When individuals participating in online learning events are separated by physical or geographic location and sometimes are working in isolated conditions, the ability to establish interpersonal contact with others greatly diminishes because all contact is electronic.

Go back to the initial scenario I described and think about this as being the normal conditions under which online participants attempt to learn. What impact would these conditions have on their ability to learn and on their desire to maintain participation? How can social presence help avoid the negative outcomes that are likely to be illustrated through a response to this question?

Before talking about the benefits of social presence and how it is established, working definitions are needed. The section to follow includes a discussion of the ways in which social presence has been defined in the literature.

Definition of Social Presence

Although the roots of social presence can be traced back to Mehrabian's concept of immediacy (as reported in Rourke, Anderson, Garrison, and Archer, 1999), much of today's application of the construct is found within the communications literature. In studying face-to-face, audio, and closed-circuit television encounters, Short, Williams, and Christie (1976) define *social presence* as the "degree of salience of the other person in the interaction and the consequent salience of the interpersonal relationships" (p. 65). As Gunawardena and Zittle (1997) suggest, intimacy and immediacy are two concepts associated with social presence in which intimacy is dependent on nonverbal factors, including physical distance, eye contact, and smiling. Immediacy is a "measure of the psychological distance that a communicator puts between himself or herself and the object of his/her communication" (Gunawardena and Zittle, 1997, p. 9). The researchers continue by postulating that immediacy or nonimmediacy can be conveyed nonverbally (that is, physical proximity, formality of dress, and facial expression) as well as verbally.

Kearney, Plax, and Wendt-Wasco (1985), Gorham (1988), and Christophel (1990) provide some of the early descriptions of the concept of social presence from an instructional communication perspective, defining it as "teacher immediacy" in the classroom. Behaviors that create immediacy include both verbal and nonverbal actions such as gesturing, smiling, using humor and vocal variety, personalizing examples, addressing students by name, questioning, praising, initiating discussion, encouraging feedback, and avoiding tense body positions (Hackman and Walker, 1990). Rourke, Anderson, Garrison, and Archer (1999) place more responsibility on the learners when they describe social presence as the ability of the learners to socially and affectively project themselves in communities of inquiry.

Others have offered the following interpretations of the concept: "the feeling that others are involved in the communication process" (Whiteman, 2002, p. 6); "the degree to which a person feels 'socially present'" (Leh, 2001, p. 110); "the degree of person-to-person awareness" (Tu, 2000, p. 1662); "the sense of being present in a social encounter with another person" (McLellan, 1999, p. 40), and "the degree to which participants are able to project themselves affectively within the medium" (Garrison, 1997, p. 6). However, Gunawardena and Zittle (1997) put it most simply when they say that social presence is "the degree to which a person is perceived as a 'real person' in mediated communication" (p. 9).

Benefits of Social Presence

The overall goal for creating social presence in any learning environment, whether it be online or face-to-face, is to create a level of comfort in which people feel at ease around the instructor and the other participants. Without this goal being achieved, the learning environment can turn to one that is not fulfilling or successful for the instructors and the learners. As Whiteman (2002) states, "People feel more comfortable around us when they believe we share a kinship and common values" (p. 8). When the environment is lacking social presence, the participants see it as impersonal and, in turn, the amount of information shared with others decreases (Leh, 2001).

As Yoon (2003) found, social behaviors accounted for 26.3 percent of the total performed behaviors by virtual learning teams. He identified these as greetings, sharing of personal life, sharing of work and professional interests, discussing the course, pairing and member support, and sharing humor. Sharing of personal life, discussing the course, and sharing of work and professional interests decreased over time, while sharing humor and pairing and member support increased over time. Yoon (2003) posits that virtual team members try early on to enhance the social presence within an online environment, and those relationships between group members gradually change from formal to informal over time. In addition, they illustrate the importance of social interaction with others within online environments.

Raising social presence in online environments may help to create impressions of quality related to the experience on the part of the student (Newberry, 2001). Social presence in learning leads to inclusion (the need to establish identity with others), control (the need to exercise leadership and prove one's abilities, and affection (the need to develop relationships with people (Whiteman, 2002). High levels of social presence create a learning environment that is perceived as warm, collegial, and approachable for all involved (Rourke and others, 1999). An additional benefit of social presence, according to Rourke and others (1999), is its ability to instigate, sustain, and support cognitive and affective learning objectives by making group interactions appealing, engaging, and intrinsically rewarding.

Gunawardena and her colleagues have produced probably the most extensive body of empirical research related to social presence and its influence in online environments. Two key studies are applicable to this discussion. In a 1997 study, Gunawardena and Zittle examined the influence of social presence as a predictor of satisfaction within computer-mediated conferencing (CMC) environments. Defining satisfaction as the value of the CMC in facilitating learning for the students, they found social presence to be a strong predictor of satisfaction in online environments. In a more recent study, Gunawardena, Nolla, and others (2001) posit that social presence facilitates the building of trust and self-disclosure within an online learning context.

As reported by Shin (2002), much of the research to date has looked at the relationship between the varying extent of social presence and the level of student satisfaction (the two primary pieces are reported in this section). In addition, other studies have examined the varying extent of social presence and the level of student learning achievement (see Shin, 2002, for this review). Although these studies hypothesize that the level of perceived social presence will produce positive effects on student learning, only research by Hackman and Walker (1990) reports a positive relationship between social presence and degree of perceived learning outcome as well as satisfaction.

Although the benefits of social presence can be seen more extensively in the area of student satisfaction, a body of literature is beginning to grow that suggests an influence on learning outcomes as well. Therefore, it is important for course designers, instructors, and participants to know how to create this social connection within learning environments. Of particular importance is to know how to create this connection in online environments due to the isolated nature of these instructional settings. The remainder of this chapter is devoted to offering strategies for creating social presence in online environments.

Strategies for Creating Social Presence

This section examines strategies that will help establish and maintain social presence within online environments. In this section, I offer strategies for the three groups of individuals involved with the three functions of these environments: (1) course designers (course design), (2) instructors (delivery and management), and (3) participants (participation). In reviewing the literature, the main responsibility for creating social presence is placed on the instructors. However, based on my personal experience as an online course designer and online course participant, I contend that the responsibility for establishing and maintaining social presence extends beyond the role of the instructor.

Course Design. Social presence should be initiated in the actual design of an online course. This section takes a look at different course design strategies that can facilitate the establishment of social presence.

Develop Welcome Messages. All online courses should include some type of welcome message from the instructor. In the courses in the online curriculum that I teach, this is actually a thirty-second streamed video in which the instructor welcomes the students, introduces himself or herself, and provides a brief overview of the course. For those without the technology to create a video, an alternative is a written welcome statement from the instructor with his or her picture included. The goal is to allow the students some opportunity to know who the instructor is prior to the start of the class and to put a face to a name.

Include Student Profiles. A second design strategy that we incorporate is to include student profiles in one of the earlier pages of the course Web site. The student profile includes a picture of the student, e-mail address(es), instant messenger ID, and a bio of approximately one page. The bio includes the student's current position, prior experience, interests associated with the field of study, and any other personal information they choose to share with the class, including hobbies and family. Because no Web site is fully secure, this is an option; students are not required to submit a picture or a bio; many just submit a bio with no picture. Any information, whether visual or written, helps both the instructor and the other members of the class build a social connection with each other. As Newberry (2001) points out, the inclusion of pictures is a low-cost option for raising social presence.

Incorporate Audio. The technology that exists today allows a close replication of a face-to-face environment at a reasonable cost to both the organization and the participants. Therefore, it is recommended that the online environment incorporate some form of audio into the design. This can be one-way audio in which the instructor broadcasts to the students or it can be two-way audio in which both instructor and students broadcast back and forth. The latter scenario does require the participant to have advanced technology, which can be costly. Because of this, my program only uses one-way audio.

Audio helps to create social presence by reflecting the emotions of the instructor to the students. It can also help establish the formality of the environment and the friendliness of the instructor and can encourage participation (McLellan, 1999). In environments in which the conversation is text-based only, there is a potential risk of someone interpreting meanings of words and statements incorrectly. This is very easy to do when the instructor is trying to type fast or accidentally has the "caps lock" function on. The use of audio helps students be at ease with the instructor.

When two-way audio is not an option, developers should examine other options for placing students' voices in the online environment (Newberry, 2001). In my department's online program, we provide a toll-free number that allows students to call in and speak with the instructor and to be broadcast to the remaining class. This gives the students an option of responding either in text form or verbally and helps them establish presence with the other members of the class as well as the instructor.

Limit Class Size. The size of the class significantly influences the establishment of social presence. Rovai (2001) suggests a student-instructor ratio of no higher than 30:1. Beyond this, the amount of social presence that can be established between students and the instructor diminishes. Class sizes in the program I teach in range from twenty to thirty students; the number is often based on the kinds of studies that make up the curriculum. A more project-portfolio-oriented curriculum may not permit as many students due to the time it takes to provide feedback on work; one that has less project-portfolio work can handle more students. With attrition rates taken into account, our course sizes usually level to around twenty-five students, which appears to be an optimum number.

Structure Collaborative Learning Activities. Collaborative learning activities can increase learner-to-learner interaction leading to social presence (Rovai, 2001, 2002; Whiteman, 2002). However, in order for these activities to work well, they need to be planned in advance. Such activities can include group work, group discussions, brainstorming, group assignments, group projects, and online group debates. In addition to creating social presence, collaborative learning activities have the potential to encourage students to search for facts and theories, thus removing the task of being the sole repository of knowledge from the instructor (Whiteman, 2002). However, as Rovai (2002) cautions, "Online instructors must ensure equal opportunities for participation by all students" (n.p.).

Instructors. Instructors play a significant role in establishing social presence for online environments. In this section, I discuss some of the specific ways in which instructors can create such an environment.

Contribute to Discussion Boards. Typically, the electronic discussion board is part of an online environment. What we as instructors often times forget is that the discussion board takes the place of the verbal discussion and interaction that occurs in a face-to-face classroom. Therefore, instructors should not be passive but should be actively involved in the discussions taking place in this medium. Not participating is the equivalent of lecturing for the entire period of a face-to-face class and then leaving without any interaction with the students. It is also the equivalent of putting students into a small-group activity and not interacting with the small group or debriefing the activity. The instructor should remember that discussion still needs to occur in these environments, and this form of interaction helps establish a social connection with all members of the class.

However, as Rovai (2001) states, "Online instructors need not reply to all learner postings to course discussion boards" (p. 290), although participants should feel that their comments are being read. Interactions must be deliberately structured in order to overcome threats to social presence. Instructors do this by "[balancing] the need for immediate responses with providing the opportunity for other members of the community to respond" (Rovai, 2001, p. 290). Those who are considered successful instructors are able to develop this sense of timing.

Promptly Answer E-Mail. Social presence is the extent to which individuals in electronic environments are perceived as real. In a face-to-face environment, participants come and meet with the instructors with questions, comments, and concerns. Consequently, there is no question as to whether or not individuals are real when they meet face-to-face. However, this is not always the case in the electronic environment. Think about times when you have sent an e-mail to someone and not received a timely response. Timely responses from instructors are valuable to the establishment of social presence in the online environment (Newberry, 2001). The technology automatically puts students at a physical distance in many instances, but instructors need to manage the process so that this distance is not an added difficulty. My rule of thumb is to answer student e-mail associated with a current class within twenty-four hours unless stated otherwise. Students need to feel that their messages are valued by the instructor and have the same amount of priority as any other message.

Provide Frequent Feedback. Feedback is critical in online courses. Participants need feedback related to areas such as assignments, participation, and their progress in the course. Whiteman (2002) recommends that this feedback be personalized and addressed to the individual student rather than given as mass feedback to the entire class. Although group feedback is needed, it's the individual feedback that establishes social presence by showing value for the student and his or her work. It may also be beneficial to check in with students on some regular schedule to determine whether there are any issues with which they need assistance.

Strike Up a Conversation. Each of our courses has roughly two hours worth of asynchronous instruction online, with a one-hour synchronous chat session each week. Although each instructor uses the synchronous chat session differently, one thing all instructors can do is strike up a conversation with students prior to officially starting class. Students typically start joining the chat about ten minutes prior to the official start time. I also try to log in early and use this time just to talk with students about anything other than the class. We talk about how everyone's week is progressing, the weather, where different people live, their families, and so on. The goal is to get to know more about each other.

Share Personal Stories and Experiences. I have found that sharing personal stories and experiences significantly facilitates social presence in online environments, basically in two ways. The first is by illustrating that the instructor is credible. Prior to taking my faculty position, I worked both as a community college administrator and a research-evaluation specialist in a Fortune 500 company. Because I am working with students in the field of human resource development and community college leadership, this brings legitimacy to me as an instructor. The second way that sharing personal stories and experiences helps is by allowing students to see that I am human and that I have had experience working in the same areas they aspire to work in or may already be working in.

Because online programs are popping up around every corner, the best ones have to establish legitimacy. One way of doing this is hiring instructors who are real, and part of conveying this "realness" is sharing these experiences.

Use Humor. This strategy is related to the one previously discussed. Although self-disclosure promotes social attraction and bonding between individuals, humor is the invitation to start a conversation (Gorham and Christophel, 1990). Humor reduces social distance and conveys goodwill within the learning environment by serving as a factor in immediacy. Obviously, all humor must be in good taste and not be of the nature that offends participants.

Use Emoticons. Emoticons are facial expressions created through the use of punctuation marks on the keyboard. Although earlier technology only allowed the use of emoticons created through punctuation, much of today's technology will translate those expressions created through punctuation into an actual facial expression. Other systems provide facial expressions from which to select, which eliminates the need for the punctuation. Emoticons help convey the nonverbal cues of the communicator, which helps participants accurately interpret the instructor's messages.

Address Students by Name. Addressing students by name creates social presence in any environment. Students' names can be more difficult to learn in an online environment because many of the nonverbal cues we typically use to assist us are gone. Often students' names appear in the list of chat participants. However, some systems are simple Net IDs (much like those used in e-mail addresses), which prevent us from knowing who the participants are. This is where the student profiles can come into play. I print out the student profiles with their pictures and have them hanging next to my computer. This allows me to glance up and associate a Net ID not only with a name but with a face. It permits me to respond to students by addressing them on a first-name basis.

Allow Students Options for Addressing the Instructor. Formal titles establish a hierarchy within social situations. There is certainly a time and place for them. However, I don't believe titles are appropriate, especially in the online environment. I feel the use of formal titles creates a distance between the instructor and the participants.

I encourage students to address me in a way that is comfortable to them. I give them the options of Dr. Aragon, Professor Aragon, Steven, Steve, Dr. Steven, Dr. Steve, or just Doc. I also add a little humor at this point and tell them they may feel the need to address me by a not-so-pleasant name by the end of the course! Titles aren't important to me in the teaching environment. I believe I can learn as much from many of the students as they do from me and possibly more. My particular titles simply acknowledge my job, which all parties already know, or indicate that I've been to school a little longer. If it makes students more comfortable to address me by one of my titles, that's fine. I simply don't want to decrease social presence by insisting on this.

Participants. Participants also need to assume responsibility for creating positive learning environments for themselves and others. In this final section, I offer suggestions to participants for facilitating social presence in the online environment.

Contribute to Discussion Boards. Just as instructors need to remember that the electronic discussion board takes the place of the verbal discussion found in a face-to-face classroom, so do the participants. Participating on a regular basis helps students get to know each other and helps the instructor get to know the students. It is very easy to be passive when it comes to discussion boards, and passivity leads to instructional and social experiences that are not fulfilling.

Promptly Answer E-Mail. Students need to remember that instructors too wonder about the "realness" of their electronic participants. I believe it is important for students to follow the same twenty-four-hour rule when interacting with their instructor via e-mail. Just as students can come to feel their messages aren't valued due to delayed responses from the instructor, the instructor can feel the same way.

Strike up a Conversation. Creating social presence is not the sole responsibility of the instructor. Therefore, participants can contribute to the social presence in their environment by initiating conversations themselves prior to the start of class. I sometimes get the feeling that students feel they should "sit quietly" on the Internet until the instructor is ready to begin. I encourage the opposite. I think it's important that camaraderie be built by all. In fact, it doesn't bother me that students have private chats with each other during the class session. If our goal is to replicate, as closely as possible, the social presence from a face-to-face environment within an online environment, we should welcome this as long as it's not distracting for others. Because of the private chat features in most communication software, the private chats aren't even visible to the instructor or other students.

Share Personal Stories and Experiences. Experiences vary across students and between the students and instructor. Students should feel comfortable sharing their own personal stories and experiences as they relate to the topic. This establishes social presence among students and with the instructor. It also contributes to active participation in the class.

Use Humor. The same rule applies to participants that applies to the instructor. Humor can do much in reducing social distance, but it should be in good taste.

Use Emoticons. Participants too should provide nonverbal cues through the use of emoticons. Many times, as an instructor, I've wondered if a posted statement was presented in anger, frustration, or any number of other emotions. Emoticons help the instructor accurately interpret participants' messages.

Use Appropriate Titles. Address the instructor by a title of identification that is comfortable to you, yet within the guidelines provided by the instructor. Addressing someone in a way you are uncomfortable with tends to decrease the level of social presence between the two of you. If the options given are not comfortable to you, talk with your instructor. Even though the options may not expand, just getting to know your instructor on a more personal basis can be helpful in establishing presence.

Conclusion

The use of online delivery as an education and training method continues to expand across various settings. For educational settings, literature provides evidence that students do not persist at the same rates as students in traditional face-to-face programs (Rovai, 2002). Although not much is known about how participants in training settings feel about the online environment, it is logical that users of this medium would want to seek ways for making the experience as enjoyable as possible. One means of doing this from the outset is through the establishment of social relations within these environments.

The strategies discussed in this chapter are not new. However, trying to establish social presence in a computer-mediated environment is no doubt more difficult to do and requires a conscious and deliberate effort on the part of the course designers, instructors, and participants. The strategies presented in this chapter may seem simple. However, from my experience of working in this environment for the past several years, they are often taken for granted. Therefore, course designers, instructors, and participants are encouraged to incorporate the strategies that are appropriate for their environments.

References

Bibeau, S. "Social Presence, Isolation, and Connectedness in Online Teaching and Learning: From the Literature to Real Life." *Journal of Instruction Delivery Systems,* 2001, *15*(3), 35–39.

Christophel, D. "The Relationship Among Teacher Immediacy Behaviors, Student Motivation, and Learning." *Communication Education,* 1990, *39,* 323–340.

Garrison, D. R. "Computer Conferencing and Distance Education: Cognitive and Social Presence Issues." In *The New Learning Environment: A Global Perspective.* Proceedings of the International Conference on Data Engineering World Conference, Pennsylvania State University, University Park, 1997.

Gorham, J. "The Relationship Between Verbal Teacher Immediacy Behaviors and Student Learning." *Communication Education,* 1988, *37*(1), 40–53.

Gorham, J., and Christophel, D. "The Relationship of Teachers' Use of Humor in the Classroom to Immediacy and Student Learning." *Communication Education,* 1990, *39,* 46–61.

Gunawardena, C. N., Nolla, A. C., Wilson, P. L., Lopez-Islas, J. R., Ramirez-Angel, N., and Megchun-Alpizar, R. M. "A Cross-Cultural Study of Group Process and Development in Online Conferences." *Distance Education*, 2001, 22(1), 85–121.

Gunawardena, C. N., and Zittle, F. J. "Social Presence as a Predictor of Satisfaction within a Computer-Mediated Conferencing Environment." *The American Journal of Distance Education*, 1997, 11(3), 8–26.

Hackman, M. Z., and Walker, K. B. "Instructional Communication in the Televised Classroom: The Effects of System Design and Teacher Immediacy on Student Learning and Satisfaction." *Communication Education*, 1990, 39(3), 196–209.

Johnson, S. D., Aragon, S. R., Shaik, N., and Palma-Rivas, N. "Comparative Analysis of Learner Satisfaction and Learning Outcomes in Online and Face-to-Face Learning Environments." *Journal of Interactive Learning Research*, 2000, 11(1), 29–49.

Kearney, P., Plax, T., and Wendt-Wasco, N. "Teacher Immediacy for Affective Learning in Divergent Colleges Classes." *Communication Quarterly*, 1985, 3(1), 61–74.

Leh, A. S. "Computer-Mediated Communication and Social Presence in a Distance Learning Environment." *International Journal of Educational Telecommunications*, 2001, 7(2), 109–128.

McLellan, H. "Online Education as Interactive Experience: Some Guiding Models." *Educational Technology*, Sept.-Oct., 1999, 36–42.

Newberry, B. "Raising Student Social Presence in Online Classes." In *WebNet 2001*. Proceedings of the World Conference on the WWW and Internet. Norfolk, Va.: AACE, 2001.

Rourke, L., Anderson, T., Garrison, D. R., and Archer, W. "Assessing Social Presence in Asynchronous Text-Based Computer Conferencing." *Journal of Distance Education*, 1999, 14(2), 50–71.

Rovai, A. P. "Building and Sustaining Community in Asynchronous Learning Networks." *Internet and Higher Education*, 2001, 3(2000), 285–297.

Rovai, A. P. "Building Sense of Community at a Distance." *International Review of Research in Open and Distance Learning*, 2002, 3. Retrieved from http://www.irrodl.org/content/v3.1/rovai.html, June 10, 2003.

Shin, N. "Beyond Interaction: The Relational Construct of 'Transactional Presence.'" *Open Learning*, 2002, 17(2), 121–137.

Short, J. E., Williams, E., and Christie, B. *The Social Psychology of Telecommunications*. New York: Wiley, 1976.

Tu, C. H. "Strategies to Increase Interaction in Online Social Learning Environments." In *SITE 2000*. Proceedings from the Society for Information Technology and Teacher Education International conference. Norfolk, Va.: AACE, 2000. (ED 444 550)

Whiteman, J.A.M. *Interpersonal Communication in Computer Mediated Learning*. (White/opinion paper). 2002. (ED 465 997)

Yoon, S. W. "Examination of Member Behaviors, Group Processes, and Development-Shaping Forces of Virtual Learning Teams." Unpublished doctoral dissertation, Department of Human Resource Education, University of Illinois, Urbana-Champaign, 2003.

STEVEN R. ARAGON *is an assistant professor in the Department of Human Resource Education at the University of Illinois at Urbana-Champaign, specializing in postsecondary education (community college), teaching and learning models for postsecondary minority and nontraditional students, and minority student development in community college settings.*

6

Assessing participant learning in online environments provides benefits and challenges. Fortunately, the available technology tools allow for a wide range of assessment techniques.

Assessing Participant Learning in Online Environments

Angela D. Benson

Assessment is a key component of any teaching and learning system. Assessment should be an ongoing process, integrated throughout the course, workshop, or program, and should consist of multiple measures, not merely a single grade provided at the conclusion of the learning event (Robles and Braathen, 2002; Shuey, 2002). Because the same data are often used to analyze student learning and to measure program effectiveness, the terms *evaluation* and *assessment* are often confused (Frederick, 2002). Reeves (2000) distinguishes the two terms by defining *assessment* as "the activity of measuring student learning and other human characteristics such as aptitude and motivation where evaluation is focused on judging the effectiveness and worth of programs and products" (p. 102). Robles and Braathen (2002) identify three key components of assessment: (1) measurement of learning objectives, (2) self-assessment for students to measure their own achievement, and (3) interaction and feedback between and among the instructor and students. Used appropriately, assessment provides helpful and much-needed guidance for learners and instructors.

Unfortunately, assessment development is an ongoing challenge for educators, whose worries range from whether their assessments are accurately measuring what they were intended to measure to whether they are fair to all learners. As instructors move to online teaching and learning environments, they face similar assessment challenges. After a discussion of assessment taxonomies, this chapter explores the benefits and challenges of assessing learning in online environments and provides a sampling of online assessment strategies and techniques.

New Directions for Adult and Continuing Education, no. 100, Winter 2003 © Wiley Periodicals, Inc.

Assessment Taxonomies

Discussions of assessment tend to follow one of two taxonomies. Hanson, Millington, and Freewood (2001) categorize assessments by purpose. They identify three categories: (1) diagnostic assessment, (2) formative assessment, and (3) summative assessment. Diagnostic assessment "provides an indicator of a learner's aptitude and preparedness for a programme of study and identifies possible learning problems" (p. 2). Formative assessment "provides learners with feedback on progress and informs development but does not contribute to the overall assessment" (Hanson, Millington, and Freewood, 2001). The goal of formative assessment is to improve teaching and learning, not to provide evidence for grading learning achievement (Rovai, 2000). Summative assessment "provides a measure of achievement or failure made in respect of a learner's performance in relation to the intended outcomes of the programme of study" (p. 2). According to Rovai (2000), summative assessment includes the awarding of grades and is "the process of gathering, describing, or quantifying information about learner performance" (p. 142).

Speck (2002) describes assessment as traditional or alternative, based on the learning domains of Bloom's taxonomy that they best measure. Traditional assessment positions learners as "recipients of knowledge [whose] function is to absorb a body of information and demonstrate that they have absorbed the knowledge by answering test questions correctly" (p. 10). Traditional assessment measures learning at the lowest levels of Bloom's cognitive domain: knowledge and comprehension (Robles and Braathen, 2002). Traditional assessments include fill-in-the-blank, true-false, matching, and multiple-choice questions. In contrast, alternative assessment positions learners as "extremely active in the process of learning . . . both encouraged and enabled to go beyond surface answers by using higher-level thinking skills of synthesis, analysis, and evaluation" (p. 11). Alternative assessment measures learning at the higher-order thinking of the cognitive domain (for example, application, analysis, synthesis, and evaluation), as well as learning that falls into the affective domain (for example, feelings, values, appreciation, enthusiasms, motivations, and attitudes). Alternative assessment embraces notions of social learning and collaboration and includes team activities, peer evaluations, self-evaluations, and portfolios.

Zeliff and Schultz (1998), in Robles and Braathen, (2002), identify a third type of assessment: performance assessment, which measures learning in the psychomotor domain. Performance assessment includes demonstrations of learner competence in a skill or task (Robles and Braathen, 2002). Reeves (2000), who considers performance assessment a type of alternative assessment rather than a new category of assessment, characterizes performance assessment as "focused on learners' abilities to apply knowledge, skills, and judgment in ill-defined realistic contexts" (p. 105). According to Reeves, there are five key attributes of performance assessment: (1) focuses on complex learning, (2) involves higher-order cognitive skills, (3) stimulates a wide range of active responses, (4) involves challenging tasks that require multiple steps, and (5) requires significant time and effort. Reeves's conceptualization of performance assessment measures learning that encompasses both the cognitive and psychomotor domains.

The two assessment taxonomies are not competing. A particular assessment may be described as diagnostic, formative, or summative, as well as traditional, alternative, or performance. The former taxonomy refers to the purpose of the assessment, whereas the latter refers to the learning domain the assessment best measures. An assessment system for a course, workshop, or program should consist of measures from multiple categories. There should be diagnostic, formative, and summative assessment in every learning event, as determined by the purpose of the learning event and the needs of the learners. Assessments should measure learning in all relevant learning domains. Because not all learning in a learning event takes place at the lower levels of the cognitive domain, then not all assessment should be concentrated at these levels.

Assessment in the Online Environment: Benefits and Challenges

The principles of assessment do not change in an online environment. In fact, assessment becomes more critical in the online environment because the environment does not allow direct observation in the way that the traditional face-to-face classroom does (Rovai, 2000). However, the technologies that underpin the online learning environment provide capabilities beyond those provided in the traditional classroom. As a result, there are benefits to assessing learning in the online environment as well as challenges.

Online Assessment Benefits. Two key benefits of online assessments are (1) the ability of every learner to respond to every question the instructor asks (Robles and Braathen, 2002) and (2) the ability of the instructor to provide immediate feedback to each learner (Wall, 2000). In a traditional course, when the instructor asks a question, the first student to answer is typically afforded the sole opportunity to provide an answer. On occasion, the instructor may ask multiple students the same question. Although important learning occurs as students listen to other students provide answers to questions, there is usually no time for every student in the class to test out his or her understanding of the concepts for feedback. This is not the case in the online environment. Using e-mail or asynchronous discussion tools, every student is allowed to respond to every question and to put forth his or her thoughts. When using asynchronous discussion tools, the online environment allows for social interaction comparable to classroom discussion in which students can build their thoughts on the thoughts of others. In contrast, when using the e-mail tool, each student has the ability to provide a fresh response, free from the influence of peers' responses.

Depending on the purpose of the assessment and the learning being assessed, one or both tools may be used.

A second key benefit to online assessment is the ability to provide immediate feedback to learners. These assessments may require the learner to complete a series of questions, after which the learner is provided with a summative grade as well as corrective feedback on each question answered incorrectly. Alternatively, the assessments may provide feedback as the learner completes each question. This feedback, for example, may provide additional information or direct the learner to related content for further study. When immediate feedback is provided automatically by the test program, it requires very little additional work for the instructor. When automatic feedback mechanisms are not provided, the instructor must provide feedback individually for each student—a time-consuming process.

Online Assessment Challenges. The key challenges to online assessment can be summed up and described in one term: *academic dishonesty* (Olt, 2002; Rovai, 2000; Shuey, 2002). This umbrella term includes issues related to learner identity and work ownership. The biggest concern for online educators is ensuring that the learner enrolled in online study is the learner who completes the coursework, including assessments. Although this issue also exists in traditional classroom courses in which the instructor does not know each student, it is exacerbated in the online environment when the instructor cannot see any of the students. Proctored testing at a site local to the learner is an often-used solution to the identity verification problem associated with major summative type assessments, for example, midterm and final exams. Possible proctored test sites include schools, libraries, churches, learning centers, and testing centers. The proctor at the test site verifies that the individual taking the test is the individual enrolled in the course. Advanced technologies based on fingerprints, voiceprints, and other unique individual traits are being developed, but these are expensive and not widely available.

Plagiarism is another component of the academic dishonesty challenge (Rovai, 2000). The Web has made finding information, copying it, and inserting it into a document very quick and easy to do. Learners can even purchase papers online. One remedy for this is to make sure that learners understand how to conduct research properly and that they understand what plagiarism is. Web sites like Plagiarism.org and Integriguard.org provide services to help educators prevent and detect plagiarism. Instructors may submit learners' work to these sites and have it checked for plagiarism.

The use of a variety of assessments during the learning event is also a way of addressing the academic dishonesty issue. The administration of multiple and varied assessments allows instructors to identify inconsistent work and alert them to the possibility of academic dishonesty (Shuey, 2002). Relying on one measure makes academic dishonesty a much easier option for learners.

Providing learners a clear description of what constitutes academic dishonesty and its penalty also serves as a deterrent because it makes learners aware of what is acceptable and unacceptable behavior in the online environment. Finally, academic dishonesty will be an issue as long as there are dishonest people in the world. Instructors in online learning environments can take steps to prevent it, but ultimately the integrity of the learners determines whether prevention is possible.

Online Assessment Strategies and Techniques

Reeves (2000) identifies three questions that educators must answer when developing assessments: (1) What is the purpose? (2) What is the scope? and (3) What is being assessed? A successful strategy that answers these questions includes a combination of diagnostic, formative, and summative assessments that range from traditional to alternative to performance, depending on the domain of the expected learning outcomes.

This section presents a discussion of eleven different assessment techniques that may be used to assess learning in the online environment: selected response assessments, constructed response assessments, virtual discussions, concept mapping, e-portfolio assessment, writing, field experiences, individual and group projects, informal student feedback, peer assessment, and self-assessment. Although many educators today have access to systems like Blackboard and WebCT that have built-in assessment tools and templates, this section includes (where appropriate) a discussion of basic HTML tools that educators who do not have access to course management systems can use to develop their own online assessments.

Selected Response Assessments. Selected response assessments include multiple-choice, true-false, and matching questions (Shuey, 2002). Assessments of this type typically measure lower-end cognitive skills, factual recall, and recognition; thus they are characterized as traditional assessment. They are subject to security and academic honesty challenges, which are typically addressed by providing a question bank that randomly selects questions for each learner each time a test is taken.

Selected response assessments are easy to respond to and easy to grade, and are the easiest to have graded electronically. They are also the easiest to construct online. Most course management systems provide tools to create tests with these items in a fairly straightforward manner. These tools allow for automatic grading of the items, as well as immediate feedback to the learner after each question is answered or after the complete set of questions is answered. Although selected response questions can be used in summative assessment, they are most effective as formative tools to provide the learner with feedback on his or her knowledge of a particular area. In self-paced, nonfacilitated online learning environments, constructed response items can be used effectively for diagnostic assessment. For example, learners can be given an online pretest that determines which sections of the full learning content they should study.

Selected response assessments can be constructed easily by using HTML forms (Sanchis, 2001). Many Web sites provide assessment construction tools that automatically generate the HTML code needed for such items, for example, http://a4esl.org/c/qw.html, http://www.connectseward.org/shs/quizcrtr/. Other sites allow instructors to create tests and maintain them on the provider's server, for example, Discovery School Quiz Center at http://school.discovery.com/quizcenter/quizcenter.html, Quiz Lab at http://www.quizlab.com/, Quiz Star at http://quiz.4teachers.org/index. php3.

Constructed Response Assessments. Constructed response assessments include fill-in-the blank, short-answer, show-your-work, and visual-depiction activities (Shuey, 2002). In these kinds of questions, students are required to create answers to questions or visual prompts. These assessments are typically lower-end cognitive, though by adding essay questions that require more detailed responses, they can address higher-order cognitive skills. The quiz generation tools that allow instructors to create selected response items also allow the creation of constructed response items. Although automatic feedback can be provided for most constructed response items, essay questions typically require an instructor to provide individual feedback to each student.

Virtual Discussions. A key feature of the online environment is the ability to conduct virtual discussions. These discussions may be synchronous (real-time) or asynchronous (delayed). Synchronous discussions occur via tools like Internet chat and instant messaging, whereas asynchronous discussions occur over Web-based bulletin boards and discussion lists. Although synchronous discussion provides social interaction that mimics the face-to-face interaction in the traditional classroom, asynchronous discussion supports high-level learning because it allows learners to formulate their ideas through thoughtful interactions with the ideas and responses from their peers. The advantage that asynchronous discussion has over synchronous discussion is the opportunity for learners to engage in thoughtful reflection before contributing to the discussion (Harasim, 1989; Rovai, 2000; Shuey, 2002). Further, classroom discussions are characterized by their pace, that is, learners have to jump in early, else the discussion may leave them behind. Not so in the online classroom. Using an asynchronous discussion list, learners can read responses from their peers during the morning hours, prepare a thoughtful response during the day, and post it that evening.

The use of rubrics can direct students toward effective participation in online discussions and make assessing that participation much easier. Rubrics establish the written criteria for assessing student performance. In general, a rubric for asynchronous discussion should include expectations for frequency of access, level of participation (for example, reads messages of others, posts message) and comprehensiveness of responses (for example, posts new ideas, synthesizes and analyzes peers' ideas, integrates with course content, stimulates discussion) (Bauer, 2002; Robles and Braathen, 2002; Rovai, 2000). Rubrics for synchronous discussions should include expected arrival time and level of participation (for example, responds voluntarily, responds when prompted, generates new ideas) (Bauer, 2002).

Concept Mapping. Concept mapping allows students "to diagram their structural comprehension of ideas and delineate the relationship among the components" (Frederick, 2002, p. 19). Conducted periodically during a period of study, concept maps can show how student comprehension changes over time (Frederick, 2002). Concept maps provide instructors with feedback on learner understanding and identify places where instructional emphasis should be placed. As such, concept maps are good formative assessment tools. Although programs like Inspiration are especially good for creating concept maps, word processing programs like Word and presentation programs like PowerPoint are just as effective.

Portfolio Assessment. A portfolio is a collection of work done by a learner over time; an e-portfolio is an electronic version of the portfolio. A portfolio serves as evidence of learner achievement in the areas covered by the portfolio. According to Frederick (2002), "Reviewing the portfolio reveals not only the solution at which the student arrives, but also the process of that journey. This takes away the focus from merely obtaining the 'right answer' and emphasizes the importance of using complex cognitive process to construct a valid solution" (pp. 19–20). Although portfolios tend to be summative, they can be done formatively, with a learner turning it in multiple times and getting feedback for improvement before submitting it for the final grade. Portfolio rubrics should address content, clarity, and style (Canada, 2002).

Writing. Writing formal papers can also be used as an assessment tool in the online environment (Frederick, 2002). These papers can be submitted via e-mail or via digital drop boxes, which are provided with most course management systems. Choosing a format like RTF (rich text format) ensures that files will be readable across most word processing programs. Substantive feedback, using word processing tools such as Track Changes and Insert Comment, can be easily provided directly into the text of the submitted document.

Field Experiences. Assessment in online environments need not be restricted to activity conducted online. Learners can and, in many cases, should engage in authentic activity in traditional face-to-face settings. These activities include internships, laboratory assignments, clinical assignments, and apprenticeships. Assessment includes performance reports from directors of field experience and evidence of student learning through portfolios, journals, and videotapes. Rubrics for field experiences should include a detailed project description, dates of the field experience, and learning expectations (Nicolay, 2002).

Problem-Solving Simulations. In lieu of field and lab experiences, simulations attempt to present the learner with authentic learning situations by integrating real-world elements into the online learning environment (Frederick, 2002). The goal of these simulations is higher-order cognitive skill and psychomotor skill development. Effective simulations guide students through the process of learning and practicing new skills and then provide opportunities for them to apply their knowledge to a variety of simulated real-life situations. When students can apply what they have learned to these situations, they provide evidence that meaningful learning has taken place.

Individual and Group Projects. Individual and group projects can provide as high-level learning for online learners as they do for classroom learners. In the online environment, group members communicate via the technology. As with classroom projects, online projects require an assessment of the project and of the group participation when the project is done by a group. Group participation rubrics should include participation in group asynchronous discussion, participation in group synchronous discussion, group project grade, participation in drafting process, and participation in a peer preview of a draft (Gray, 2002). Projects can be prepared for presentation on the Web via videotape that is mailed to the course instructor or by using photographs. If the nature of the project permits, it can be mailed to the course instructor.

Individual and group projects tend most often to be used as summative evaluation. The components of the rubric for individual and group projects include project description, project due dates and milestones, and learning expectations (Nicolay, 2002).

Informal Student Feedback. The online environment provides rich and easy methods of obtaining informal feedback on individual student progress. In class-paced, instructor-facilitated learning environments, instructors can use the one-sentence summary or minute paper in which students provide a summary of the main points of the lesson or unit as formative assessment ("Better Assessment . . .," 2002). Each of these strategies provides a way for instructors to get brief feedback from every learner. The instructor can use this information to provide structure for future learning. For example, if these assessments show that students do not grasp a topic, instructors may direct learners to additional study materials for that topic.

Peer Feedback. Peer feedback is also an effective assessment technique to use in the online environment (Levin, Levin, and Waddoups, 1999). For example, learners can share drafts of writing projects and obtain feedback from each other. When learners are provided with rubrics to structure their feedback, it becomes an opportunity for higher-level learning. In addition, with rubrics learners can also grade each other's projects.

Self-Assessment. Opportunities for self-assessment can be valuable to learners. Levin, Levin, and Waddoups (1999) use a form of self-assessment in which they, as instructors, post previous classes' assignments on the Web and allow students to compare their work to the exemplary work of others.

Conclusion

Assessment in the online environment has challenges and benefits. The key challenge is the issue of academic honesty; the key benefit is the ability to provide immediate feedback to students. Fortunately, the availability of online technology tools allows for the development and use of a variety of assessments. These assessments may be for diagnostic, formative, or summative purposes. Using traditional, alternative, and performance assessment, instructors may assess learning in the cognitive, affective, and psychomotor domains. When assessing higher-order cognitive learning, it is important that learners be provided rubrics to detail expected performance. Assessment techniques useful in assessing learning in an online environment include selected response assessments, constructed response assessments, virtual discussions, concept mapping, portfolio assessment, writing, field experiences, individual and group projects, informal student feedback, peer assessment, and self-assessment.

References

Bauer, J. F. "Assessing Student Work from Chatrooms and Bulletin Boards." In *New Directions for Teaching and Learning,* no. 91. San Francisco: Jossey-Bass, 2002.

"Better Assessment Key to Student Learning." *Online Classroom,* July 2002, p. 3.

Canada, M. "Assessing E-Folios in the On-Line Class." In *New Directions for Teaching and Learning,* no. 91. San Francisco: Jossey-Bass, 2002.

Frederick, P. "The Need for Alternative Authentic Assessments in Online Learning Environments." *Journal of Instruction Delivery Systems,* 2002, 16(1), 17–20.

Gray, R. "Assessing Students' Written Projects." In *New Directions for Teaching and Learning,* no. 91. San Francisco: Jossey-Bass, 2002.

Hanson, J., Millington, C., and Freewood, M. "Developing a Methodology for Online Feedback and Assessment." Paper presented at the Fifth International Computer Assisted Assessment Conference, Leicestershire, U.K., 2001.

Harasim, L. "On-Line Education: A New Domain." In R. Mason and A. Kaye (eds.), *Mindweave: Communication, Computers and Distance Education.* Oxford: Pergamon Press, 1989.

Levin, J., Levin, S., and Waddoups, G. "Multiplicity in Learning and Teaching: A Framework for Developing Innovative Online Education." *Journal of Research on Computing in Education,* 1999, 32(2), 256–269.

Nicolay, J. A. "Group Assessment in the On-Line Learning Environment." In *New Directions for Teaching and Learning,* no. 91. San Francisco: Jossey-Bass, 2002.

Olt, M. R. "Ethics and Distance Education: Strategies for Minimizing Academic Dishonesty in Online Assessment." *Online Journal of Distance Learning Administration,* 2002, (3), http://www.westga.edu/%7Edistance/ojdla/fall53/olt53.html.

Reeves, T. C. "Alternative Assessment Approaches for Online Learning Environments in Higher Education." *Journal of Educational Computing Research,* 2000, 23(1), 101–111.

Robles, M., and Braathen, S. "Online Assessment Techniques." *Delta Pi Epsilon Journal,* 2002, 44(1), 39–49.

Rovai, A. P. "Online and Traditional Assessments: What Is the Difference?" *Internet and Higher Education,* 2000, 3(3), 141–151.

Sanchis, G. R. "Using Web Forms for Online Assessment." *Mathematics and Computer Education,* 2001, 35(2), 105–113.

Shuey, S. "Assessing Online Learning in Higher Education." *Journal of Instruction Delivery Systems,* 2002, 16(2), 13–18.

Speck, B. W. "Learning-Teaching-Assessment Paradigms and the Online Classroom." In *New Directions for Teaching and Learning,* no. 91. San Francisco: Jossey-Bass, 2002.

Wall, J. E. *Technology-Delivered Assessment: Diamonds or Rocks?* ERIC/CASS Digest. Greensboro, N.C., 2000.

Zeliff, N., and Schultz, K. *Authentic Assessment in Action: Preparing for the Business Workplace.* Little Rock, Ark.: Delta Pi Epsilon, 1998.

ANGELA D. BENSON *is an assistant professor in the Department of Human Resource Education at the University of Illinois, Urbana-Champaign. She teaches and conducts research in instructional technology.*

7

Basing their remarks on personal experience, two recent graduates of an online master's degree program share their insights on this educational technology from the consumer's perspective, including benefits, challenges, and recommendations for students and institutions.

Meeting the Needs of Consumers: Lessons from Postsecondary Environments

Herbert E. Huber, Jean C. Lowry

As most practitioners in the adult learning arena are well aware, distance learning has been around for a long time. However, with advances in computer technology over the last several years, the Internet has become the primary delivery medium. Institutions of higher education have taken advantage of this to expand the availability of their programs, particularly at the graduate level. For example, the Web site for Geteducated.com, an e-learning consulting firm, indicates that there are over 160 graduate programs offering postbaccalaureate distance learning master's degrees, doctorates, and advanced career certificates in business, management, and administration, including more than 90 accredited distance learning MBAs, with 43 of these accredited by the Association to Advance Collegiate Schools of Business International. More than 80 accredited graduate programs offer postbaccalaureate, advanced certificates in technology, computer science, Internet commerce, engineering, manufacturing, and other areas of distance learning. In addition, more than 60 accredited graduate programs offer post-baccalaureate degrees in distance learning and advanced certificates in education or library science and media specialties (Geteducated.com, 2003).

Traditional programs will probably never go away, but the process of learning is changing. Many institutions use online courses as a component of their programs but retain a requirement for the student to complete part of the coursework in-residence. However, there appears to be a move toward fully online degree-granting programs, as both public and private universities redefine their "market" in global terms. A recent study found that more

New Directions for Adult and Continuing Education, no. 100, Winter 2003 © Wiley Periodicals, Inc.

than 350,000 students were enrolled in fully online degree-granting programs in 2001-02, generating $1.75 billion in tuition revenues for the institutions involved. The study also notes that the market for fully online degree programs is growing at a rate of 40 percent annually (Gallagher and Newman, 2002). The question then becomes, What does an institution that wants to gain a share of this growing market need to do to ensure the success of its online programs?

Best Practices

The following eight regional accrediting commissions have developed a list of best practices and protocols for electronically offered degree and certificate programs:

1. Commission on Higher Education, Middle States Association of Colleges and Schools
2. Commission on Institutions of Higher Education, New England Association of Schools and Colleges
3. Commission on Technical and Career Institutions, New England Association of Schools and Colleges
4. Commission on Institutions of Higher Education, North Central Association of Colleges and Schools
5. Commission on Colleges, The Northwest Association of Schools and Colleges
6. Commission on Colleges, Southern Association of Colleges and Schools
7. Accrediting Commission for Community and Junior Colleges, Western Association of Schools and Colleges
8. Accrediting Commission for Senior Colleges and Universities, Western Association of Schools and Colleges

The New England Association of Schools and Colleges (NEASC) divides the best practices into five separate components: (1) institutional context and commitment, (2) curriculum and instruction, (3) faculty support, (4) student support, and (5) evaluation and assessment. These criteria are intended to assist institutions in planning online programs and provide a benchmark to those institutions already offering online programs.

NEASC notes that these are not new evaluative criteria. Rather, they reflect how criteria already well established in regional accrediting standards apply to online programs (New England Association of Schools and Colleges, 2003). Our personal experience in the HRE Online program at the University of Illinois at Urbana-Champaign (UIUC) supports this assertion.

Institutional Context and Commitment. Education is best experienced within a community of learning where competent professionals are actively and cooperatively involved with creating, providing, and improving the instructional program. Our experience with HRE Online certainly supports this assertion. Our first exposure to the program was through its Web site, which gave us a good indication of the institution's ability to use technology in the learning environment. The site was well designed and very informative, and the staff continued to make improvements to it over the three years we were in the program. During the course of the program, we were impressed with the level of communication, cooperation, and teamwork exhibited among instructors in the program, as well as among instructors and their teaching and technical assistants. It was clearly evident that mentoring relationships existed within the department.

We also found that the design of the program facilitated the "community of learning" concept. The HRE Online program organizes around learning cohorts, which are groups of students who enroll at the same time and move through the program together, taking the same courses at the same time. Research on learning in cohorts indicates that cohorts foster a sense of belonging, create an environment of mutual respect, promote risk taking, provide a forum for critical reflection and shared understanding, and encourage and sustain multiple perspectives. As a result, cohort members have positive feelings about their experiences (Imel, 2002). That was certainly our experience in the HRE Online program.

Curriculum and Instruction. Learning is dynamic and interactive, regardless of the setting in which it occurs. There are indications that online instruction can be as effective as other methods, specifically face-to-face learning, but may not be suitable for courses that require a high degree of student-instructor interaction (Johnson, Aragon, Shalik, and Palma-Rivas, 2000). The determining factor is how the curriculum designer integrates sound learning principles into the online learning environment (Johnson and Aragon, 2002). Our experience supports this assertion.

In the HRE-Online program, extensive interaction occurred in both synchronous and asynchronous sessions that created a virtual classroom. In the synchronous sessions, the instructor, teaching assistant, and technical support staff normally controlled the classroom. Live one-way audio, in this case using a commercially available streaming audio application, enabled students to hear the instructor and staff members during the session. Using the multitasking capabilities of today's PC operating systems that allow multiple windows to be open, students could also view the slide presentation for the session and participate in a course chat room. The chat room permitted students to interact in real-time with the instructional staff and other cohort members, make comments, and read comments from classmates. Both the audio transmission and the chat room discussion were archived and the files made available for review on the course Web site—a big plus for those of us who had to miss a class session.

Another level of interaction took place "behind the scenes," as students used instant messaging applications to carry on private discussions. Often referred to as "passing notes in class," it could be as distracting in the virtual classroom as side discussions in the traditional classroom. However, these discussions did not distract the instructional staff, who were unaware of this activity in their virtual classroom. Interaction in the asynchronous portion of the courses usually took the form of posting information on a course Web board or exchanging e-mail. We were extremely pleased with the level of interaction throughout the entire three years of the program.

Faculty Support. Instructional programs leading to degrees having integrity are organized around substantive and coherent curricula, which define expected learning outcomes. The nine courses that make up the HRE Online program are the same courses offered to on-campus students pursuing a master's in global HRD. At times during our program, we had on-campus students enrolled in our online course when their schedule would not permit attending an on-campus class. The direct implication here is that the UIUC views online courses as equal to traditional, on-campus offerings. A standard practice for instructors in the HRE Online program at UIUC is to provide a detailed course syllabus that is published on the Web site for the course. The syllabus served as a road map for the course, defining expected learning outcomes and describing specific course requirements and grading criteria. This proved to be a valuable resource for us.

Student Support. Institutions accept the obligation to address student needs related to their academic success and to provide the necessary resources. We found this to be especially true in the online learning environment. Research indicates that online students need certain technical knowledge and skills to successfully participate in online programs (Johnson, Palma-Rivas, Suriya, and Downey, 1999). Institutions offering online programs should provide the necessary training to the student before and during their participation in online programs. Technical support should also be available to the students. UIUC met this obligation in the HRE Online program by clearly stating on its Web site what knowledge and skills a student should possess to participate in the program. Students were also required to complete an online orientation program that familiarized them with some of the software they would use in the program and the instructional design format that was used consistently throughout the curriculum.

In addition and perhaps most important, the program provided a technical support staff. The staff for each HRE Online course included the instructor, a teaching assistant, and one or more technical assistants knowledgeable in the applications used. All were present for each class. If needed, technical assistance was available via telephone, FAX, e-mail, and instant messaging. The HRE Online technical support staff was accessible via instant messaging, e-mail, and telephone seven days a week to provide technical assistance if needed. Many of us took advantage of this support and felt it was a strength of the program.

Evaluation and Assessment. Institutions undertake the assessment and improvement of their quality, giving particular emphasis to student learning. Almost all institutions conduct assessments of their programs. However, it is what they do with the information that really counts. We were asked to complete an end-of-course evaluation after each course. At first, many of us were skeptical that anything would be done with our evaluations, but most of us were pleasantly surprised to see that our comments and suggestions did have an impact. We were able to see changes from one course to the next, based on our recommendations. As the program progressed, we became more comfortable at giving "right now" feedback about the program and about how to improve our learning experience. The administrators listened and sometimes were able to implement changes during a course. One suggestion that we offered—(and were extremely pleased when it was implemented)—was the appointment of a "student advocate"— a staff member whose function was to be the "single point of contact" in the communication process between the students and the HRE Online administration. We felt this facilitated the communication processes.

What Makes a Successful Online Instructor?

Even when an institution follows the best practices, the impact of the learning experience relies heavily on the online instructor. The Illinois Online Network Web site lists several criteria for a successful online instructor that coincide with our own experience (Illinois Online Network, 2003).

Have Broad-Based Life Experience. Instructors should have a broad base of life experiences in addition to academic credentials. Literature supports the notion that knowledge is in part a product of the context in which is it developed and used. One of the best ways to promote contextual learning in the online environment is to simulate reality using appropriate case studies (Johnson and Aragon, 2002). Our experience was that the instructors who could best provide real-life examples were those who had a basis of practical experience outside academia, either as employees or as consultants. Some of our better instructors were the program's adjunct professors who were either consultants or employees of a business. They were active HRD practitioners and taught college part-time because they wanted to, bringing a wealth of experience to the classroom on how to apply concepts in the real world, which they willingly shared with us.

Be Open and Flexible. The instructor's personality should demonstrate the characteristics of openness, concern, flexibility, and sincerity. A benefit of online learning that makes it so attractive to older students with full-time jobs is the ability to participate in class from any location with Internet access. However, this benefit also creates conflicting priorities. Most of our HRE Online cohort were working professionals who had to juggle the demands of their job, family, and classwork. Sometimes class had to take second place. Flexible and understanding instructors and staff helped students make the most of these difficult situations.

Possess Good Communication Skills. The instructor should be comfortable communicating in writing. The face-to-face contact found in traditional classroom settings does not exist. The communication exchange is now conducted primarily via keyboard. From our experience, the pace is often intense and demanding, and the best instructors are those best able to communicate in writing—a fundamental skill in the online learning environment.

Be a Proponent of Online Learning. The instructor should be a proponent of facilitative learning, seeing it as equal to the traditional model. Our cohort experience increased the value of the degree. Learning occurred not only from self-study and the instructor's sharing of knowledge and experiences but from members of the cohort who challenged our ideas and provided insight based on their experiences. Some of our most valuable synchronous sessions were those in which the instructor initiated a structured discussion related to that week's content, then assumed the role of facilitator as cohort members explored, interpreted, and challenged the content from our various perspectives.

Value Critical Thinking. The instructor should value critical thinking as a part of the learning process. By design, the online learning environment requires students to use reflective observation (learning by watching and listening) and abstract conceptualization (learning by thinking), simply because of the way course materials are organized and delivered (Aragon, Johnson, and Shaik, 2002b). To facilitate both, HRE Online instructors used a variety of techniques that included organizing courses around projects. For example, both the Instructional Systems Design course and the instructional technology course had major individual course projects, whereas major projects in other courses required a team initiative. Instructors also used small-group discussions during synchronous sessions and required students to complete short writing assignments on a particular topic as a means of assessing learning.

Be Trained in Online Instruction. The instructor should be experienced and well trained in the online learning experience. Our experience is that the characteristics of an effective online program are not necessarily synonymous with those of a classroom program. Consequently, competencies of a classroom instructor do not directly correlate with those of an online instructor. Online instructors must develop new instructional skills (primarily related to the use of technology), as well as refine and augment existing skills (feedback, communication, innovation, and courseware design, among others). The educational institution can assist instructors new to online programs by providing training in the technology, introducing innovative instructional strategies, and offering suggestions for adapting classroom teaching methods to the online environment.

What Should Students Expect from the Instructor?

Responsibility for learning should be shared between the instructor and the student. Just as the instructor has specific expectations for the student, the student can and should have certain expectations of the instructor. The business experience that several of us in the cohort possessed led us to a customer service perspective on our expectations of the instructor. In other words, we tended to view the instructor as a service provider and ourselves as the customers. To us, satisfaction with the program was very important, and how well the instructor met our expectations contributed significantly to our satisfaction. Based on our experience, the student should expect the instructor to do the following:

• *Create a learning environment that uses work, life, and educational experiences to make the learning meaningful and relevant.* Relevancy was critical to maintaining student motivation within our cohort.

• *Present the material in a way that facilitates translating theory to practice and application.* As adult learners, we wanted to be able to apply what we were learning. In fact, many of the course projects were developed with work-related circumstances and actually implemented after the course was over.

• *Solicit and listen to feedback.* Instructors should be attuned to concerns and suggestions about the course, instruction, staff, and support functions. They should take action when appropriate to improve the program and be willing and able to explain why suggestions can't be implemented.

• *Provide timely and constructive feedback on the students' efforts.* Several members of the cohort were self-proclaimed overachievers with a high need to know what they could do to improve their performance. Regardless of our self-perceptions, we all wanted to know how we were doing. The courses we were most disappointed with were those where feedback from the instructor was lacking.

• *Keep students informed on the status of course requirements.* Give regular updates on what is due, what has been turned in, and what is missing. This simple act helps give students a sense that they have some degree of control by helping them manage priorities.

• *Be readily available to answer student questions and address student concerns.* HRE Online instructors accomplished this by establishing regular online "office hours," when they would monitor instant messenger sites or Web boards, as well as respond promptly to e-mail messages.

What Makes a Successful Online Student?

The student in the online program shares responsibility for the success of the learning process. According to the Illinois Online Network Web site (Illinois Online Network, 2003) and our own personal experience, a successful online student should be able to do the following:

• *Be able to meet the program's minimum requirements.* The requirements for an online program are no lower than for any other quality educational program. The admissions requirements and procedures into UIUC's HRE Online program were the same as the on-campus program. Our expectation was that participating in the online program would be more convenient than the on-campus program, not easier. We weren't disappointed.

• *Have access to and a minimum proficiency in the use of the necessary hardware and software.* By its very nature, online distance learning is dependent on technology. UIUC established the minimum hardware and software requirements needed for a student to be able to participate in the program. Anything less severely hampered the student. We would compare it to a student trying to complete a traditional course without using pen and paper. It also seemed to us that individual success in any course was influenced by the student's level of proficiency. In addition, we found the level of student frustration to be dependent on the student's proficiency with the hardware and software. Generally, those who were comfortable with the hardware and software seemed to do better in the program.

• *Be able to communicate through writing.* The majority of interaction with the instructional staff and with teammates and cohort members is in writing. Much of that writing is in a chat room format, which requires rapid keyboarding and quick development of thoughts in a clear, concise format. Often this occurs while listening to the instructor's lecture and reading classmates' comments as they scroll across the screen. Therefore, the ability to multitask is a critical skill for the student.

• *Be self-motivated and self-disciplined.* Research supports our contention that the student's level of motivation affects the level of learning (Aragon, Johnson, and Shaik, 2002a). We believe our cohort was successful because the members wanted to be in the program, not because they had to. The primary reason people gave for dropping out of the program was that their personal goals and priorities changed. The second major reason was that they got behind in the work and could not finish the course requirements. It was very apparent to us that success also depended on our personal self-discipline.

• *Be willing and able to commit sufficient time per week to coursework.* Pursuing an advanced degree requires a significant commitment, whether one selects a traditional program or one offered online. The initial information we received from the university said to expect to spend ten to fifteen hours per week with the HRE Online program. In fact, the time required was on the high side of this range. At times, we found ourselves spending more than twenty hours online, not including the time working on assignments when we were not online.

• *Be willing to speak up if problems arise.* We found that the distance format increased a sense of isolation; instructors and classmates were invisible, and you didn't have the ability to incorporate body language or tone into written communication. If you didn't speak up, you could quickly get left behind, and the instructor might not detect your problem until it was too late. The student must accept responsibility for learning and take the initiative when necessary with instructors and with teammates.

• *Accept critical thinking and decision making as part of the learning process.* Because of the design of online courses, critical thinking and decision making are essential elements of the learning process (Aragon, Johnson, and Shaik, 2002b). Instructors encouraged us to self-critique and provide constructive feedback to others. Courses were organized around real-world projects that required us to decide how to apply concepts and theory presented in class. Working in virtual teams initially posed some problems for us, but deciding how to resolve these issues enriched the overall learning experience.

• *Be open-minded about sharing experiences as part of the learning process.* As we indicated earlier, context is an essential central element in learning (Johnson and Aragon, 2002). We found that one of the best ways to place learning in context was through shared examples from experience. Several members of our cohort were active HRD practitioners who brought a wealth of experience to the program. More important, they were willing to share their experiences with the cohort and thereby expanded the opportunity for learning for everyone.

Conclusion

Online learning is having a tremendous impact on the education process in schools, universities, and corporate settings. As technology continues to develop, this delivery method will increase in quality and quantity. Consumers should be cautioned, however, that all online programs are not of equal quality, and they should carefully evaluate each program.

From our perspective, the experiences that led to our graduate degree in HRD were as meaningful and valuable as any we would have received as an on-campus student. Our learning experience increased in value as we developed new competencies by using the learning technologies. We believe that online learning provides experiential learning in the course content, as well as the learning technologies and supports the development of new skills and character traits that are beneficial in all areas of life.

References

Aragon, S. R., Johnson, S. D., and Shaik, N. "A Preliminary Analysis of Learning Style Influence on Student Success in Online vs. Face-to-Face Environments." In B. Cope and M. Kalantzis (eds.), *Learning for the Future.* Melbourne, Australia: Common Ground Publishing, 2002a.

Aragon, S. R., Johnson, S. D., and Shaik, N. "The Influence of Learning Style Preferences on Student Success in Online vs. Face-to-Face Environments." *American Journal of Distance Education,* 2002b, 16(4), 227–243.

Gallagher, S., and Newman, A. "Distance Learning at the Tipping Point: Critical Success Factors to Growing Fully Online Distance-Learning Programs." *Eduventures.* Boston, 2002. Available from https://www.eduventures.com/research/industry_research_resources/distancelearning.cfm.

Geteducated.com. Essex Junction, Vt., 2003. Available from http://geteducated.com.

Illinois Online Network. Champaign, Ill., 2003. Available from http://www.ion.illinois.edu/IONresources/onlineLearning/index.asp.

Imel, S. "Adult Learning in Cohort Groups" (practical application brief no. 24). Columbus, Ohio: ERIC Clearinghouse on Adult, Career, and Vocational Education, 2002. Available from http://ericacve.org/docgen.asp?tbl=pab&ID=114.

Johnson, S. D., and Aragon, S. R. "An Instructional Strategy Framework for Online Learning Environments." In T. M. Egan and S. A. Lynham (eds.), *Proceedings of the Academy for Human Resource Development*. Bowling Green, Ind.: Academy for Human Resource Development, 2002.

Johnson, S. D., Aragon, S. A., Shalik, N., and Palma-Rivas, N. "Comparative Analysis of Learner Satisfaction and Learning Outcomes in Online and Face-to-Face Learning Environments." *Journal of Interactive Learning Research*, 2000, *11*, 29–49.

Johnson, S. D., Palma-Rivas, N., Suriya, C., and Downey, S. "Examination of Critical Issues for Development and Implementation of Online Instruction." Department of Human Resource Education, University of Illinois at Urbana-Champaign, 1999. Available at http://www.hre.uiuc.edu/online/issues.pdf.

New England Association of Schools and Colleges (NEASC), Commission on Institutions of Higher Education. *Best Practices for Electronically Offered Degree and Certificate Programs*. Bedford, Mass.: NEASC, 2003. Available at http://www.neasc.org/cihe/best_practices_electronically_offered_degree.htm.

HERBERT E. HUBER is the manager of Performance Improvement for Temple-Inland Forest Products Corporation in Diboll, Texas, and holds a master's in education in global human resource development from the University of Illinois at Urbana-Champaign.

JEAN C. LOWRY is the manager of employee development for Energen Corporation in Birmingham, Alabama, and holds a master's in education in global human resource development from the University of Illinois at Urbana-Champaign.

8

*This chapter discusses the current environment of online
learning in business and industry, followed by a case study
from one of Intel Corporation's training organizations.*

Meeting the Needs of Consumers:
Lessons from Business and Industry

Lisa A. Garrett, Connie L. Vogt

Human resource development (HRD) initiatives are used by business and
industry as a means of improving the workplace performance of employees.
Online learning using the Internet and computer technology is one tool that
is significantly altering how training and development initiatives are being
delivered. Within business and industry, globalization, advances in technology,
shifting demographics, economic change, and the ever-increasing need for
skilled workers have cultivated an environment that is receptive to online
learning. Companies that need to develop employees at sites around the world
have used online learning as a way to provide consistent, equitable training.

Advances in computer and networking technologies have allowed business and industry to support learning by expanding training approaches and
engaging learners in new ways. Companies are seeking efficient ways to train
their employees and see online learning as a tool that is geared to the needs
and interests of the individual learner. Online learning has shown potential for
reducing the costs of workplace-related education and training.

The chapter begins by describing the current environment for online
learning, followed by a discussion of the benefits and challenges of using
online instruction in business and industry. Two issues affiliated with online
learning, blended learning and standards, are highlighted. The chapter ends
with a case study of a manufacturing organization's experience with online
learning.

The Current Online Learning Environment

Although many companies can claim to report admirable cost savings and
increases in productivity due to online learning, other companies are still

NEW DIRECTIONS FOR ADULT AND CONTINUING EDUCATION, no. 100, Winter 2003 © Wiley Periodicals, Inc.

struggling with how to make online learning effective (Croft-Baker, 2001). Concern over high attrition rates among e-learners, the high cost of implementing online learning, and the lack of standards are all problems that must be dealt with.

Several trends are fueling the growth of corporate learning and the adoption of online learning (Moe and Blodget, 2000). These trends include

- A shift to a skilled workforce, along with a skills shortage among workers
- The widening wage gap between high school and college graduates
- The fast pace of technological change and shortening product life cycles
- Increased globalization
- The changing perception of corporate learning from its being a cost to being an investment

Technology-intensive industries, employers demanding relevant skills, and employees seeking opportunities for advancement and career development are creating an environment for the growth of online learning in business and industry. Various initiatives in the current business environment have also fueled the demand for online learning. More and more companies are engaging in enterprise resource planning and implementing complex systems to manage the planning. Organizations have a greater interest in knowledge sharing and in knowledge-management systems, which can become integral components of online learning. As reported by Wentling, Waight, and Kanfer (2000), McCrea, Gay, and Bacon corporate learning and the corporate learning organization have a strategic position in the context of managing and growing enterprises. E-commerce requires companies to maintain networks of customers and suppliers, which involves the responsibility of educating those customers and suppliers about products and processes. Online business practices have led business and industry to online learning.

According to the American Society for Training and Development's (ASTD) *State of the Industry Report 2001,* the percentage of organizations using the Internet for training purposes grew from 3 percent in 1996 to 38 percent in 1999. For intranets, the growth rate was from 3.5 percent to nearly 40 percent. As the use of online learning continues to grow, it's beneficial to look at ways in which online learning is used.

How On-Line Learning Is Used in Business and Industry

Online learning is used for situational learning, just-in-time learning, collaborative team learning, and scenario training. Online learning has also benefited specific organizations within a company that have geographically dispersed employees, such as sales organizations.

One of the first areas that received attention from online learning was sales training. Companies with extensive sales organizations have struggled with how to provide ongoing training and product information to geographically dispersed salesforces. Traditional instructor-led training has been the norm. Salespeople were expected to attend multiday training sessions at a company headquarters, adding up significant training costs. Now that companies have the option to provide online learning, salespeople receive consistent, immediate training. One example is MetLife Financial Services (MLFS) (Rossi, 2001). MLFS's training and development organization needed to find a method to deliver learning to a dispersed salesforce. MLFS sales reps were required to prepare for mandated examinations and had to learn new-product and procedural information in a timely manner. An online learning delivery system was developed that would allow sales reps the opportunity to access interactive, real-time classes on their laptops.

In addition, online learning is being used as a method to deliver simulation training. Simulation training is an effective tool, especially for training that would otherwise be too costly or hazardous to provide (Jackson, 2001). One example re-creates a simulated technology manufacturing plant where students start as new employees in a warehouse division as shipping and receiving clerks, move next to materials handling, and finish as material assemblers building and testing electronic equipment (Jackson, 2001). FedEx (Douglas, 2003) uses computer simulations to teach couriers to complete airway bills. Couriers learn the skill online and then practice in a classroom with real labels.

Companies are also turning to online learning to provide training to customers and supplier partners. Educating customers can provide benefits to a company in the form of increased customer satisfaction and increased sales. Companies are recognizing the importance of their partners' success and are discovering that they can extend their learning process to partners through online learning. This improves partner relationships and deepens the commitment between companies. It can also help in the development of consistent standards across partnerships (PrimeLearning, 2001).

Major strategic initiatives have served as an impetus for the use of online learning. The implementation of enterprise resource planning (ERP) and customer resource management (CRM) processes have led major learning efforts. As the number of companies undergoing implementation and upgrading of these processes continues, they are searching for online learning platforms to support training (Galagan, 2000). PriceWaterhouseCoopers built a learning platform to support an ERP upgrade that included the installation of SAP (an ERP software package), I2 (a supply chain package), and Siebel (a CRM package). The online learning platform combined a learning management system and a learning portal with SAP's content management system (Galagan, 2000). As companies continue to find ways to use online learning, they are becoming more adept at its design and implementation. But making online learning available to employees isn't enough. Companies want to know if the learning is effective, and the only way to know that is by evaluation.

The Evaluation Challenge

Evaluation of online learning still challenges business and industry. Evaluation is necessary for demonstrating that online learning is worth the effort.

An effective evaluation plan is an integral component of a successful online learning program. Organizations want proof that an investment in online learning will improve productivity and will ensure that learning has occurred; the measurement of ROI has become a concern on corporate leadership. As stated in a research report by Merrill Lynch (2000), the 1999 ASTD study of corporate training directors found that "tangible ROI results" was the number-one criterion for choosing a learning provider of online learning. Online learning ROI is an important issue within companies, and training departments are given the task of measuring the impact of online learning (Harris, 2003).

In ASTD's *A Vision of E-Learning for America's Workforce* (2001), it is recommended that new measures be developed for assessing and evaluating the effectiveness of online learning. These measures should be outcome-based, with less emphasis on utilization and completion rates. The most common variables used for measuring the effectiveness of online learning include learner satisfaction, technology satisfaction, measuring learner outcomes, and cost-effectiveness (Wentling, Waight, and Kanfer, 2000).

Measuring learner satisfaction involves measuring the level of participation and interaction, the feedback that a learner receives, the actual learning environment, and the learning environment. Measuring technology satisfaction looks at how the different components function together. These functions include the delivery method, how well the tool supports the learner, and the look and feel of the interface design (Wentling, Waight, and Kanfer, 2000).

When measuring learner outcomes, each learner's instructional objectives should be considered. Self-evaluations, pre- and post-tests, exams, peer evaluations, tracking completion times, and automatic recording of learner data are all methods that have been used for measuring learner achievement (Wentling, Waight, and Kanfer, 2000).

In measuring cost-effectiveness, Wentling found that significant financial savings are associated with the use of technology-based instruction, but cost savings should not be the only measure of effective training. Besides measuring hard cost savings such as in travel, materials, and administrative time, there are also more difficult measurements to consider (Harris, 2003). Improved productivity, employee retention and morale, and shorter learning curves can also be relevant measurements. There are no standard formulas, but these measurements should be given consideration when planning for evaluation.

In order for online learning to be successful, evaluation must play a role. It is one of the important success factors for online learning.

Success Factors for Business and Industry

In addition to evaluation, several other factors influence the success of online learning in business and industry. These include (1) organizational culture, (2) partnerships with IT, (3) links to business strategy, (4) management involvement, and (5) the effort to meet learner needs.

Organizational Culture. Before any discussion can take place regarding what factors are necessary for online learning to be successful, organizational culture must be considered. Learning should be a priority, and an organization's values and culture should support it. Online learning alone will not create a learning organization (Galagan, 2001).

An organization's culture guides behaviors and decision making. For online learning to succeed, organizational culture must support employee self-directedness (Wentling, Waight, and Kanfer, 2000). Employees won't be sitting in a traditional classroom; they may be participating in learning at their desks or at home. The open exchange of information and sharing of expertise is central to a supportive organization culture.

Rewarding and recognizing online learning and knowledge sharing are also common behaviors in an organizational culture that supports online learning. So is providing incentives and marketing to keep learners engaged (Weaver, 2002).

Partnerships with IT. Top management in an organization may not see their own training department as a key player in the development of online learning initiatives and often turn to the IT department (Barron, 2000; Weaver, 2002). If a training organization is to be successful with online learning, it's important to recognize the value of partnering with IT. The IT department can provide expertise on the impact that online learning has on the organization's technology systems. They can help decide which tools and which infrastructure to use. Partnering helps avoid the situation of the training organization developing something that meets a business need but can't be technologically implemented or the IT department designing something that meets a technical need but is inadequate for learners. At Cisco Systems, the IT department and the Internet Learning Solutions Group partnered to implement online learning solutions. Company leaders believe this partnership is one of the key factors affecting the success of their online learning initiatives (Galagan, 2002).

Links to Business Strategy. Online learning should be a key component of a company's business strategy. For online learning to succeed, it has to be linked to the specific business results that an organization is trying to achieve. These results could be a successful new-product introduction, increased customer satisfaction, improved productivity, or decreased safety incidents. A training organization needs to have an understanding of business strategies and be involved in strategic planning.

Management Involvement. Along with being aligned to business strategy, online learning must also have the active engagement of senior stakeholders. The involvement of senior management ensures that employee learning is a component of the overall strategic plan. Online learning doesn't involve just technology decisions. It has to account for culture issues, leadership decisions, business challenges and trends, and long-term business results (Galagan, 2001).

ASTD's "E-Learning: If We Build It, Will They Come?" study (2001) revealed that opportunity remains for stronger manager support of online learning. Without manager support, the learner doesn't see the value of the course. The study suggests that a manager can play an essential role in supporting online learning by

- Explaining why the course should be taken
- Linking the course content to business objectives and future career opportunities
- Displaying an interest in online learning and giving it the same status as attending a classroom course
- Helping transfer the learning to the workplace
- Assigning peers to provide support

Efforts to Meet Learners' Needs.   Completing a thorough needs analysis is the first step in understanding the learning and performance needs of the learner. An analysis can ensure that the content of the online learning will address the performance gaps of the learners. Learners may need to develop new skills in order to participate in online learning. Along with being familiar with using a computer and browsing, learners may also need to be prepared to be more self-directed learners. These issues can be identified and planned for during the analysis.

For the learner, online learning must be easy to use, engaging, personalized, and customized and must provide high-quality content (Moe and Blodget, 2000). Providing learners the opportunity for interaction and collaboration is critical. Chat rooms and threaded discussions can provide opportunities for interaction. Tutors and mentors can also add value (Moe and Blodget, 2000).

Organizations can increase participation and satisfaction in online learning by providing learners the time and space to learn on company time (American Society for Training and Development, 2001). Examples of ways an organization demonstrates its support for meeting the needs of learners include providing an environment in which peer support is widespread, making the effort to provide synchronous and collaborative courses, and tying career advancement to online learning.

Johnson and Aragon (2002) offer a number of principles for making online environments effective for the learners. They suggest that the learning environment should (1) address individual differences, (2) motivate the student, (3) avoid information overload, (4) create a real-life context, (5) encourage social interaction, (6) provide hands-on activities, and (7) encourage student reflection.

Organizations should consider these success factors when planning for online learning. The absence of one or more of these factors could have an impact on the effectiveness of an online learning program.

Trends in Online Learning

Along with being aware of various success factors, it's important for organizations to be informed about trends in online learning. Two widely discussed trends at this time are (1) blended learning and (2) the adoption of standards.

Blended Learning. One trend that is discussed a great deal in the current literature is blended learning, that is, a combination of multiple learning formats and methods. Traditional instructor-led learning can be combined with online learning. This trend recognizes that online learning will not replace all other forms of learning. The benefit of blended learning is that training organizations can be creative in developing learning experiences that will satisfy the needs of a wider variety of learning styles (Taylor, 2002). The key to successful blended learning lies in selecting appropriate delivery methods for specific learning outcomes and effectively combining diverse learning events (Valdez, 2001).

Wyeth Pharmaceuticals (Click2Learn, 2002) developed a blended learning program for their salesforce that combines online lessons, readings, and one-to-one training. This training covered new-employee orientation topics such as company procedures, product information, selling technique, and regulations. New salespeople received the training online and in face-to-face mentoring sessions. This type of blended learning provides more opportunity for personal interaction, collaboration, and feedback.

Adoption of Standards. For online learning to become more accessible, consensus will have to be reached on shared technical standards. One of ASTD's recommendations in the report *A Vision of E-Learning for America's Workforce* (2001) is to "adopt common technical standards aimed at promoting open and equitable access while reducing development costs" (p. 23). Common standards will enable communications among different platforms, operators, providers, sites, and individuals. Standards can also help reduce the time and cost of production, customize instruction, and easily transfer materials across technology (American Society for Training and Development, 2001). Online learning professionals believe that the development of standards will be the most critical factor in the success and adoption of online learning (Taylor, 2002).

One solution to the standards issue has been SCORM. As an initiative of the United States government, the Sharable Content Object Reference Model (SCORM) was developed as an attempt to furnish a set of common specifications and standards for technology-based learning. The intention of SCORM is to provide recommendations for consistent implementations of technology-based learning by the vendor community; some parts affect vendors for learning management systems and content-authoring tools, as well as instructional designers, content developers, and training providers (Advanced Distributed Learning, 2002). As SCORM and other standards continue to expand and become more refined, the expectation is that there will be more integration and interoperability of online learning technology.

It is evident that online learning will remain a primary method for facilitating learning in organizations. Consequently, the more we can learn from practitioners in the field, the better we can understand the trends and the impact that online learning has on HRD initiatives.

In the section to follow, one of the authors shares her experience from a corporate training management perspective as to how online learning has made, and continues to make, changes to the training delivery landscape.

Intel Corporation's Technical Training

One of Intel Corporation's computer microchip manufacturing facilities successfully implemented an online delivery, learner evaluation, and tracking process using a component of their existing learning management system. The results yielded significant gains in cost-efficiency for labor and for improvement in measurements of learner competency.

Company Profile. Founded in 1968, Intel Corporation supplies the computing and communications industries with chips, boards, systems, and software building blocks that are the "ingredients" of computers, servers, and networking and communications products. Intel is a leader in semiconductor manufacturing and technology and has established a competitive advantage through its scale of operations, agility of its factory network, and consistent execution worldwide. Intel has twelve fabrication facilities (Fabs) and twelve assembly and test facilities worldwide.

Situation: Need for Greater Cost and Learning Effectiveness. Challenging economic times for the technology industry from 2001 to the present led Intel's computer-chip-making Fab in Colorado to look for greater cost-and-learning effectiveness in its delivery of technical procedural change training. In the fast-paced, high-tech manufacturing environment, critical changes to work procedures for technicians and engineers occur frequently. Consistent understanding and application of new knowledge and skill across multiple shifts with regard to safety, equipment operations, and quality-enhancing procedures is essential to cost-effective production. In addition, there were increased time pressures demanding that procedural change training reach the target audience, usually consisting of hundreds of technicians who were working shifts across a 24/7 schedule.

Intel's network of Fabs provided extensive training and a robust certification process for technicians, including a blend of formal classroom training, Web-based training courses, and structured on-the-job training for new hires and existing employees moving to new job functions as a result of promotions and turnover. The Colorado Fab took pride in the quality, rigor,

Figure 8.1. Technical Training Change Request: Traditional Methods

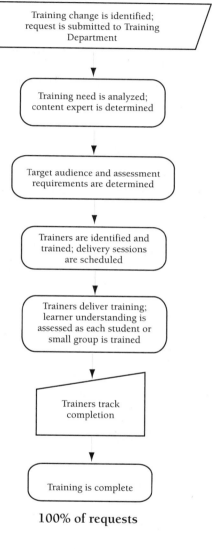

Training change is identified; request is submitted to Training Department

Training need is analyzed; content expert is determined

Target audience and assessment requirements are determined

Trainers are identified and trained; delivery sessions are scheduled

Trainers deliver training; learner understanding is assessed as each student or small group is trained

Trainers track completion

Training is complete

100% of requests

Change is involved:
- Training trainers
- Face-to-face training sessions
- Logistical challenges for trainees trying to balance work demands with less flexible training session schedules

and results achieved through their initial training and certification process; they had no intention of allowing a weak postcertification skill and knowledge transfer process to dilute the results of the initial training or negatively affect performance.

Ensuring that changes to existing procedures were identified and taught and that the learning was evaluated to ensure basic competency had always been a labor-intensive process. The process was bogged down by a great deal of face-to-face delivery time, variability in trainer assessment of learner understanding, and time spent tracking completion status. Although the training content was critical to ensuring quality performance, the actual delivery itself was often very brief, taking only fifteen to twenty minutes to deliver, with rarely a need for clarifying questions, yet required hours of logistical preparations to bring trainer and learner face-to-face. This process is illustrated in Figure 8.1.

Solution: Online Usage Strategy. Intel's Colorado Fab needed an improvement to its procedural change training process, providing cost, time, and learner effectiveness. The Fab's existing certification tracking database, a component of a larger learning management system, provided easy access to employee certification records, including levels of certification, job types, and shift alignments, as well as interfaces to e-mail, Web sites, and servers. In addition, the target populations were very comfortable with accessing online information and navigating Intel's intranet environment, as well as using other e-learning products such as Web-based training courses and simulations.

The Fab's training department categorized the procedural change training into two primary types. The first type required knowledge and skills training, two-way interaction (questions-answers) between trainer and learner, and hands-on practice or demonstration of learning. The second type required a transfer of knowledge and few-to-no questions from the learner (one-way exchange to the learner). Both categories required tracking status and completion, as well as assessment of learner understanding.

An analysis of past procedural training change types indicated that approximately 80 percent of the training fell into the latter, one-way exchange category. It became clear that if technicians and engineers could access the training content, they could self-administer the training; face-to-face time and the corresponding logistics weren't really necessary.

Because the certification tracking system interfaced with existing communication systems, it was modified to notify any specific target audience via e-mail that a "self-administered" training session for a procedural change was available to them and required completion within a specified timeframe. Upon receiving the e-mail, the employee would access the certification tracking system, where an online training session could be accessed (a variety of software applications could be used, depending on the content and training objectives); once the training session was completed, a brief assessment was administered. Successful completion of the assessment was required before the system granted "credit" for training and updated the employee's

Figure 8.2. Technical Training Change Request: Online Enhancement

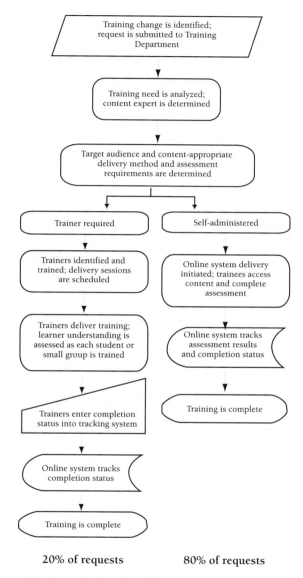

20% of requests   80% of requests

Only changes involving the need for two-way
communication or actual demonstration and/or
practice of skills involved:
• Training trainers
• Face-to-face training sessions

Changes requiring primarily one-way procedural
training with knowledge assessments to ensure
understanding involved:
• Self-administered, online training modules available
when the time is convenient for the learner

training history as complete. This new online enhancement process is represented in Figure 8.2.

It took a few months for the technicians and engineers to become familiar and comfortable with this new online method, but once established, enthusiasm for the process grew rapidly. Supervisors saw efficiency gains as technicians accessed their training change information when it was convenient for them instead of having to schedule their work around a training session taught face-to-face. Once a training change was released, it was available to the entire target population immediately, with no scheduling challenges. Finally, the online assessment feature ensured that every learner had indeed understood the core content, reducing the variability of trainer-to-trainer assessment results.

Results. The use of the self-administered versus the traditional face-to-face delivery categorization provided substantial gains in efficiency and reductions in labor costs (see process flow comparisons)—approximately $430,000 in the first year alone. The consistency provided by the use of an online learner evaluation linked to completion tracking reinforced a focus on learner competency as an objective rather than a mere completion of training. In addition, the exploitation of a previously unused feature within the existing learning management system was viewed as role-modeling cost and effectiveness results. Due to the efficiency and quality successes of this program, a number of other Fab training organizations view the process as a best practice and are currently reviewing implementation plans for their respective sites.

Conclusion

Technology has altered the way training and development is delivered in business and industry. The various benefits of online learning have influenced the increasing use of online learning methods. As organizations address the challenges of online learning, better evaluation methods and standards will be developed. The future success of online learning will depend on being a key component of the organization's strategy. Organizations must have a supportive culture, partnering abilities in those involved in implementing online learning, and management involvement, and must ensure that the needs of the learners are met.

References

Advanced Distributed Learning (ADL), 2002. "SCORM Overview." Retrieved from http://www.adlnet.org/index.cfm?fuseaction=scormabt&cfid=10678&cftoken=61455926, May 13, 2003.

American Society for Training and Development and The Masie Center. "E-learning: 'If We Build It, Will They Come?' Executive Summary," June 2001. Retrieved from http://www.masie.com/masie/researchreports/ASTD_Exec_Summ.pdf, Apr. 9, 2003.

American Society for Training and Development and the National Governors Association. "A Vision of E-Learning for America's Workforce: Report of the Commission on

Technology and Adult Learning," June, 2001. Retrieved from http://www.masie.com/masie/researchreports/ELEARNINGREPORT.pdf, Apr. 9, 2003.

Barron, T. "Getting IT Support for E-Learning." *Training and Development,* Dec. 2000, 54(12), 32–37.

Click2learn, Inc. "Wyeth Sales Training Case Study." Bellevue, Wash.: Click2Learn, 2002. Retrieved from http://home.click2learn.com/case_studies/wyeth.pdf, Apr. 8, 2003.

Croft-Baker, N. "Eight Companies Keep E-Learning from E-Scaping." *New Corporate University Review,* Mar.–Apr. 2001, 9(2). Retrieved from http://traininguniversity.com/tu_pi2001ma_4.php, Apr. 13, 2003.

Douglas, M. "E-volution at Corporate U." *E-Learning Magazine,* Jan. 2003. Retrieved from http://www.elearningmag.com/elearning/content/printContentPopup.jsp?id=43978, Apr. 14, 2003.

Galagan, P. A. "The E-Learning Revolution." *Training and Development,* Dec. 2000, 54(12), 25–30.

Galagan, P. "14 Things CEOs Should Know About E-Learning." *Training and Development,* Nov. 2001, 55(11), 69–72.

Galagan, P. "Delta Force." *Training and Development,* July 2002, 56(7), 21–31.

Harris, P. "ROI of E-Learning: Closing In." *Training and Development,* Feb. 2003, 57(2), 31–35.

Jackson, M. "Simulating Work: What Works." *E-learning Magazine,* Oct. 2001. Retrieved from http://www.ltimagazine.com/ltimagazine/article/articleDetail.jsp?id=36879, May 17, 2003.

Johnson, S. D., and Aragon, S. R. "An Instructional Strategy Framework for Online Learning Environments." In T. M. Egan and S. A. Lynham (eds.), *Proceedings of the Academy of Human Resource Development.* Honolulu: Academy of Human Resource Development, 2002.

Moe, M. T., and Blodget, H. "The Knowledge Web, Part 4: Corporate E-learning: Feeding Hungry Minds." New York: Merrill Lynch and Global Securities Research and Economics Group, Global Fundamental Equity Research Department, May 23, 2000. Retrieved from http://www-rcf.usc.edu/~ghentsch/kw4.pdf, Apr. 15, 2003.

PrimeLearning, Inc. "eLearning: A Key Strategy for Maximizing Human Capital in the Knowledge Economy" (a white paper). New York: 2001. Retrieved from http://www.primelearning.com/approach/pdf/maximizinghumancapital.pdf, Apr. 8, 2003.

Rossi, N. "Learning at MetLife Goes Virtual." *Learning Circuits,* May 2001. Retrieved from http://www.learningcircuits.org/2001/may2001/rossi.html, Apr. 2, 2003.

Taylor, C. "The Second Wave." *Training and Development,* Oct. 2002, 56(10), 25–31.

Valdez, R. "Blended Learning: Maximizing the Impact of an Integrated Solution" (a white paper). Bellevue, Wash.: Click2Learn, Inc., 2001. Retrieved from http://home.click2learn.com/en/solutions/white_papers.asp, Apr. 8, 2003.

Weaver, P. "Preventing E-Learning Failure." *Training and Development,* Aug. 2002, 56(8), 45–50.

Wentling, T., Waight, C., and Kanfer, A. "E-Learning: A Review of Literature," 2000. Retrieved from http://learning.ncsa.uiuc.edu, Apr. 16, 2003.

LISA A. GARRETT is a graduate student in the Human Resource Development program at the University of Minnesota.

CONNIE L. VOGT is manager of Fab 11 training at Intel Corporation, Rio Rancho, New Mexico.

INDEX

Robles, M., 69, 70, 71, 75, 77
Rogers, C. R., 15, 18
Rossi, N., 91, 101
Roster page, 53
Rourke, L., 59, 60, 61, 68
Rovai, A. P., 57–58, 63–64, 67, 68, 70, 71, 72, 74, 75, 77
RTF format, 75
Rubrics, assessment, 74–75
Rule of Seven, 37
Russell, T. L., 32, 43

Saffo, P., 30
Sales training, 90–91
Sanchis, G. R., 74, 77
SAP, 91
Schramm, 32
Schultz, K., 70, 78
Schunk, D. H., 16, 18
Screen design, 54
Security, student profiles and, 62
Selected response assessments, 73–74
Self-assessment, 76
Self-directiveness, 93
Self-disclosure: instructor, 64–65; student, 66
Self-efficacy beliefs, 5, 11, 13–15
Self-motivation and self-discipline, 86
Settings, traditional versus online, 19–21, 32–33, 45–46, 51. See also Online environments
Shaik, N., 1–2, 4, 32, 42, 57, 68, 81, 84, 86, 87, 88
Sharable Content Object Reference Model (SCORM), 95–96
Shin, N., 61, 68
Shoemaker, J., 32, 43
Short, J. E., 59, 68
Shuey, S., 69, 72, 73, 74, 77
Siebel, 91
Sikora, A. C., 6, 18
Simulations: for contextual learning, 38; for corporate training, 91; problem-solving, 75–76; radio talk show, 36
Size, class, 63
Small-group discussions, 40–41
Smeaton, A., 32, 43
Smith, G. G., 46, 47, 50, 55
Snow, K., 31, 42–43
Social-constructionist theories, 33
Social isolation, 58–59, 86
Social learning: assessment of, 70; instructional design for, 38–39

Social learning theory, 33, 38–39; instructional design for, 38–39; in instructional strategy framework, 34–42
Social presence, 3, 57–67; benefits of, 60–61; course design for, 62–63; definition of, 59–60; importance of, 58–59; instructors' role in creating, 63–66; strategies for creating, 61–67
Southern Association of Colleges and Schools, 80
Speck, B. W., 70, 78
Standards, adoption of, 95–96
State of the Industry Report 2001 (ASTD), 90
Steiner, V., 8, 18
Strategic organizations, 27–28
Student advocate, 83
Student-instructor ratio, 63
Student needs analysis, for corporate online programs, 94
Student profiles, online, 62, 65
Student satisfaction: with corporate online programs, 92; with face-to-face versus online instruction, 1; measurement of, 92; social presence and, 61
Students, 19; addressing, by name, 65; criteria for successful, 85–87; expectations of, for instructors, 84–85; guidelines for, on technology selection, 24–26; instructor relationship with, 39; social presence of, strategies for creating, 66–67; support for, 26, 49, 51, 52, 53, 82
Success, in online environments: learning style preferences and, 1–2; research on, 1–2; self-efficacy and, 13–14
Summative assessment, 70, 71, 73, 76
Supply partners, online training for, 91
Support. See Instructors; Organizational support; Students; Technical support
Suriya, C., 82, 88
Suzuki, K., 35, 42
Syllabus, 52–53, 82
Synchronous teaching and learning: assessment in, 74–75; defined, 8; delivery challenges of, 51; interaction in, 21, 23–25, 40–41, 64, 81–82; small-group discussions during, 40–41. See also Interaction; Online instruction and learning

Back Issue/Subscription Order Form

Copy or detach and send to:

Jossey-Bass, A Wiley Company, 989 Market Street, San Francisco CA 94103-1741

Call or fax toll-free: Phone 888-378-2537 6:30AM – 3PM PST; Fax 888-481-2665

Back Issues: Please send me the following issues at $29 each
(Important: please include ISBN number with your order.)

_____

_____

_____

$ _____   Total for single issues

$ _____   SHIPPING CHARGES: SURFACE   Domestic Canadian

	First Item	$5.00	$6.00
	Each Add'l Item	$3.00	$1.50

For next-day and second-day delivery rates, call the number listed above.

Subscriptions: Please __start __renew my subscription to *New Directions for Adult and Continuing Education* for the year 2_____at the following rate:

U.S.	__ Individual $80	__ Institutional $160
Canada	__ Individual $80	__ Institutional $200
All Others	__ Individual $104	__ Institutional $234
Online Subscription		__ Institutional $176

**For more information about online subscriptions visit
www.interscience.wiley.com**

$ _____   Total single issues and subscriptions (Add appropriate sales tax for your state for single issue orders. No sales tax for U.S. subscriptions. Canadian residents, add GST for subscriptions and single issues.)

__ Payment enclosed (U.S. check or money order only)
__ VISA __MC __AmEx __# _____ Exp. Date _____

Signature _____ Day Phone _____
__ Bill Me (U.S. institutional orders only. Purchase order required.)

Purchase order # _____
          Federal Tax ID13559302   **GST 89102 8052**

Name _____

Address _____

_____

Phone _____ E-mail _____

For more information about Jossey-Bass, visit our Web site at **www.josseybass.com**

**NEW DIRECTIONS FOR
ADULT AND CONTINUING EDUCATION
IS NOW AVAILABLE ONLINE AT WILEY INTERSCIENCE**

What is Wiley InterScience?

Wiley InterScience is the dynamic online content service from John Wiley & Sons delivering the full text of over 300 leading scientific, technical, medical, and professional journals, plus major reference works, the acclaimed *Current Protocols* laboratory manuals, and even the full text of select Wiley print books online.

What are some special features of Wiley InterScience?

Wiley InterScience Alerts is a service that delivers table of contents via e-mail for any journal available on Wiley InterScience as soon as a new issue is published online.
Early View is Wiley's exclusive service presenting individual articles online as soon as they are ready, even before the release of the compiled print issue. These articles are complete, peer-reviewed, and citable.
CrossRef is the innovative multi-publisher reference linking system enabling readers to move seamlessly from a reference in a journal article to the cited publication, typically located on a different server and published by a different publisher.

How can I access Wiley InterScience?

Visit http://www.interscience.wiley.com

Guest Users can browse Wiley InterScience for unrestricted access to journal Tables of Contents and Article Abstracts, or use the powerful search engine.
Registered Users are provided with a *Personal Home Page* to store and manage customized alerts, searches, and links to favorite journals and articles. Additionally, Registered Users can view free Online Sample Issues and preview selected material from major reference works.
Licensed Customers are entitled to access full-text journal articles in PDF, with select journals also offering full-text HTML.

How do I become an Authorized User?

Authorized Users are individuals authorized by a paying Customer to have access to the journals in Wiley InterScience. For example, a university that subscribes to Wiley journals is considered to be the Customer. Faculty, staff and students authorized by the university to have access to those journals in Wiley InterScience are Authorized Users. Users should contact their Library for information on which Wiley journals they have access to in Wiley InterScience.

ASK YOUR INSTITUTION ABOUT WILEY INTERSCIENCE TODAY!

DATE DUE

AUG 0 8 '05			
MAY AUG 7 2012			